HAUNTED CROWN POINT, INDIANA

HAUNTED CROWN POINT, INDIANA

JUDITH TOMETCZAK

Haunted America

Published by Haunted America
A Division of The History Press
Charleston, SC
www.historypress.net

First published 2017

Manufactured in the United States

ISBN 9781467136914

Library of Congress Control Number: 2017940926

For my grandson, Tyler Joshua Michael Crandall,
who loves for me to tell him scary stories.

They say that shadows of deceased ghosts
Do haunt the houses and the graves about.
Of such whose life's lamp when untimely out,
Delighting still in their forsaken hosts.

—Joshua Sylvester

CONTENTS

ACKNOWLEDGEMENTS

With the composition of my first book, I've come to realize just how much is dedication and how much is inspiration. I was given the opportunity to merge two of my passions in life, history and the supernatural, and present them in such a way to both intrigue and terrify the reader.

I was sincerely delighted to find out how much the citizens of Crown Point love their city and are eager to share their memories, experiences and secrets. Having undertaken this project has caused me to reflect on how many wonderful people have touched my life to make it possible, for without them, these pages would be blank.

My grandmother Mary Kasprzycki told me my first ghost story when I was about five years old. We used to walk along a stretch of property in Hegewisch, Illinois, that was never developed. All that was left of the project was broken and uneven concrete sidewalks. It was our favorite place, where she shared tales of local legends and restless spirits. I looked forward every Sunday to our special time together at the place she called "crooked sidewalk."

I am tremendously grateful for the constant encouragement and guidance of my two daughters, Pamela and Lisa.

Beginning with my favorite landmark in town, I found myself in the office of Martha Wheeler, president of the Lake Court House Foundation, on a cold afternoon in November. I received not only motivation from her but also an enormous amount of information about the Grand Old

Lady. Her exuberance and affection for Crown Point, as well as the historic Crown Point Courthouse, truly make her a regal matriarch.

The Indiana Room at the Crown Point Library was my second home for almost a year while I rifled through pamphlets, searched hundreds of newspaper archives and unshelved almost all of Crown Point's historical books. My gratitude to Jeanene Letcher and Laurie McDermott in the reference department for their untiring assistance.

Four astute teachers who are members of the Crown Point High School Alumni Association took the time to meet with me and give me the insight I needed to write my chapter on the haunted high school. Thanks to Bud Bowman, Marion Kellum, George Tachtiris and Dick Gordon.

Many thanks to the owner of the house on Ruffle Shirt Hill for sharing her home and her intriguing experiences with me.

Lake County historian Bruce L. Woods supplied me with valuable firsthand information regarding Crown Point, as well as remarkable photographs.

Memories are priceless. They transport us to a time and place in our past, encouraging us to recall events filled with emotions. I truly appreciate the memories of all of you who were kind enough to share them with me.

Finally, thanks to my husband, Dave, who burned the midnight oil with me and never let the lamp go out.

CHAPTER 1

THE GRAND OLD LADY

As you travel south from Route 30 on Taft Street, one of the first things you will encounter on your journey to the quaint town of Crown Point, Indiana, is the welcome sign. It reads "Welcome to Crown Point: Hub of Lake County." It is given that title because of its location, surrounded by Merrillville to the north, Winfield to the east, Cedar Lake to the southwest, St. John to the west and unincorporated Schererville to the northwest. It is at this point that Taft is renamed Main Street, a benevolent name bestowed upon hundreds of streets across our nation. This street does, however, warrant that title, because as you make your way farther down the road, you are greeted by the oh so regal Crown Point Courthouse. She stands tall and proud, surrounded by quaint antique shops, specialty shops and numerous businesses, in the very center of town, known as the Square.

Confirming her position as the foundation of Lake County, the courthouse, fondly named the "Grand Old Lady," depicts the architecture of the Victorian period, which made for a most interesting combination of Romanesque and Georgian styles. Soaring toward the sky are her triple regal towers. Center stage is the clock tower that has kept track of time since 1878, never missing a minute. Flanking the clock tower are two sister towers that complement her and appear as if they are guarding the citizens of Crown Point, who go about their daily routines far below.

The history of this admirable structure and the land on which she stands dates back to the last day of October in 1834, when Solon Robinson emerged from a thicket of woods and gazed upon miles and miles of open land. What he imagined as an opportunity of wealth and accomplishment became just that and eventually led to the creation of Lake County and the founding of Crown Point. Never before occupied by the white man, this vast expanse of prairie was quite secluded. Neighboring this region were many Potawatomi Indians who had not yet settled into reservations. Robinson and his wife, Mariah Evans, of Philadelphia, Pennsylvania, and their two children, Josephine and Solon Oscar, claimed the land of Crown Point and established their homestead on the northwest corner of what is now the Crown Point Square. It became known as "Robinson's Prairie." They soon opened their residence to aid travelers and many soon-to-become settlers, newly arrived.

The year 1837 was a busy one for Solon and his brother, Milo. They opened a store well stocked with supplies, used for trade with both the Indians and the settlers, their best customers being the Potawatomis. One of Robinson's priorities was setting land aside specifically to be used as a public square, and it was on this land that he soon constructed a small log cabin. This two-story structure cost him $500 to build and served as the very first courthouse. Even as early as 1834, the Square, then called the "Courthouse Yard," was a favorite place for the townspeople to gather and children to play. Often you could hear their young voices crying out with joy and excitement as they engaged in a raucous game of hide-and-seek. In 1868, this small area, now known as Crown Point, became a recognized community due to its continuous increase in population and businesses.

By 1849, the log cabin courthouse had outlived its usefulness, and a second courthouse was constructed on the north side of the town square at a cost of $10,000. Besides being the courthouse, the new building also housed the sheriff's office and a single jail cell in the basement.

The third and final courthouse, which graces the Square today, was built in 1878. It was more conducive to the now prominent and growing town of Crown Point. The architect, J.C. Cochran of Chicago, soon designed the structure, and a contract was signed by Thomas and Hugh Colwell from Ottawa, Illinois, to complete the building for the cost of $52,000. Half a million hand-kilned bricks were donated by Henry Wise, who was a schoolteacher in Lake and Porter Counties before he formed his brickyard company in Crown Point. Wise is buried with honor in the historical Maplewood Cemetery in Crown Point and is commemorated in a wall mural at Colonel John Wheeler Middle School, showing him in his sergeant's uniform and depicting construction of the old courthouse. It took only one year to finish, and the historical landmark was dedicated in 1880.

Solon Robinson's residence, 1836, where the first court was held, Crown Point. *Courtesy of the Lake Courthouse Foundation.*

The "Grand Old Lady" began as a place of public service to handle simple legal disputes and decide on civil and political matters. Marriage licenses were issued there, and the rotunda hosted wedding ceremonies. As time moved forward, the town welcomed its growth in county government. The economy was booming. The oil industry was started by John D. Rockefeller, and the region was becoming host to the steel mills by Judge Elbert Gary, making the Calumet Lake County region one of the greatest industrial regions of the world. A decision was made to enlarge the building by adding north and south towers for $160,000. Construction began in 1907, and once again, it was dedicated in 1909. The Crown Point Courthouse has seen many changes to its original beginnings; its last addition came in 1928, with a north and south single story, at a cost of $80,000.

Many infamous people and worldwide celebrities have graced the steps and halls of the Lake County Courthouse. William Jennings Bryan, secretary of state for President Woodrow Wilson, addressed the citizens of Lake County on October 7, 1896. He gave his speech from the courthouse steps, vying for their votes for United States president and drawing a staggering crowd.

Grand Old Lady, Crown Point Courthouse, 1878. *Courtesy of Lake County, Indiana Historical Society.*

Left: Construction crew at the Lake County Courthouse, 1878. *Courtesy of Calumet Regional Archives, Indiana University Northwest.*

Below: William Jennings Bryan addressing the citizens of Crown Point from the Lake County Courthouse, October 7, 1896. *Courtesy of the Lake Courthouse Foundation.*

Crown Point had no waiting period to obtain marriage licenses and became *the* place to wed. It became known as the "Marriage Mill" in the 1920s and hitched movie stars such as Rudolph Valentino and Tom Mix. Heavyweight champion of the world Muhammad Ali also chose to tie the knot here, and online sources claim that even Ronald Reagan and Jane Wyman came here to say "I do."

After decades and decades, is it any wonder that the walls of the Crown Point Courthouse, steeped in history and emotion, hold the secrets of the past and perhaps have a story or two to tell? Legends and eyewitness accounts of hauntings concerning it abound in the Calumet region, so much so that several paranormal groups and avid ghost hunters still use their investigative talents and techniques to satisfy their curiosity and record factual evidence to support the accounts of restless spirits.

The most intriguing legend takes us back to the American gangster era associated with organized crime and Prohibition during the 1920s and '30s. It has been rumored that several tunnels were once constructed under the streets of the Crown Point Square, originating from the cellars of several businesses and making the Crown Point Courthouse their destination. These tunnels are rumored to have been used to transport illegal alcoholic beverages during Prohibition, as well as serve as secret passageways for chosen travelers. Stories have even been told of tunnels that once transported the deceased discreetly from local mortuaries and funeral homes to the courthouse for funeral services. Although no official substantiation of these tunnels was obtained, it is a fact that at least one of these paths still exists, probing some twenty feet into complete darkness and sealed in mystery.

The courthouse was placed in the National Register of Historic Places on May 17, 1973. Once a building is placed in this honored register, its physical appearance cannot be altered. Dr. David R. Hermansen, professor of architecture and planning at Ball State University and noted authority on historical buildings in the state of Indiana, was quoted referring to it as "the most significant building in Lake County."

Ascending the limestone steps on the east side, opening the double wooden doors and crossing the threshold into a breathtaking rotunda truly transports the visitor back in time. The entrance is said to be guarded by the spirits of the past courthouse, and on several occasions, access has been denied by locking the doors, if only for a brief moment. To the right of the foyer is the office of the Lake Courthouse Foundation, where you will find the dedicated and admirable president of the foundation, Martha Wheeler. Martha—or Marty, as she is fondly referred to—devotedly oversees all aspects of

Lake County Courthouse, 1960s. *Courtesy of the Lake Courthouse Foundation.*

maintaining and operating the Crown Point Courthouse. Working in her quaint office, surrounded by photographs and memorabilia from the old courthouse, as well as bulletproof windows from when the sheriff's office once existed here, she has had her own experiences with the courthouse ghosts. She says, "I have heard lots of strange noises at night, when I'm here alone. I feel a little creepy! I've never actually seen a ghost myself, but others have noticed the ghosts and have told me about many strange happenings."

Perhaps it is the spirit of John Brown, the president of the First National Bank of Crown Point, who cordially pays Wheeler a random visit. After all, his desk, circa 1882, was donated to the Lake Courthouse Foundation and sits right in front of her.

The south half of the historical courthouse, once the offices of the prominent county treasurer and county officer, has been beautifully transformed into the elegant Maki Ballroom. Rightly named after Gunnar Maki, a major contributor to the restoration of the building, the ballroom has been host to several wedding receptions, meetings and performances.

This elegantly designed ballroom has the capacity to seat two hundred people, and guests are shined upon by nineteen sparkling chandeliers. At least one dazzling bride still makes her appearance gliding across the dance floor, as if manipulated by an unearthly breeze, clothed in an ethereal gown of white chiffon. Many guests, as well as regular courthouse employees, have seen her when the ballroom gives way to the midnight hour. She appears alone, unaccompanied by her partner. Is she unwilling to move on, or does she simply desire to dance to an eternal melody?

If you happen by any of the local residents of Crown Point and ask them about their endeared courthouse on the Square, they will undoubtedly tell you about the most famous ghost that inhabits the clock tower. Taking the elevator to the highest floor is a shaky and slow climb. Once the doors open, your eyes are immediately drawn to the enormously tall windows and seasoned surroundings. The Crown Point City Court is in session here on Tuesdays, hearing cases involving misdemeanors, traffic tickets and city ordinance violations. The City Court clerk's office is just to the right of the courtroom. An uncapacious hallway leads to a steep climb up well-trodden wooden stairs, ending with the door to the clock tower. For years, the clock tower has been restricted to visitors, as well as the curious ghost hunter, and limits any admission with wrought-iron bars. Is this gate trying to keep a ghostly spirit from escaping the ominous clock tower? Well, on at least one occasion, this obstruction has failed, because looking closely you will notice that two of the bars have been pulled apart. Stories revolving around the clock tower include seeing an apparition of a tall man in a dark coat and top hat, antecedent of an earlier time, ascending the clock tower stairs. He seems to be intent on his purpose, completely unaware of his observers. Tom, who works all hours at the courthouse as a security guard and provides maintenance for the Grand Old Lady, has had many experiences that surely denote the clock tower is home to at least one lingering spirit. Maintaining the lights that illuminate the clock face atop the façade calls for Tom to frequent the bell tower, even into the witching hours. On many occasions, he has found himself replacing the lights. After a job well done, as he exits the tower, the lights completely turn off, leaving Tom steeped in darkness. He has even seen the light switch that operates the lighting of the clock tower move on its own, as if guided by an unseen host.

Although the Lake County Government Complex, also located in Crown Point, is home to the circuit court, superior court and juvenile court, the old Crown Point Courthouse still serves its purpose by hearing misdemeanor cases. It has been extensively renovated since its original usage. The courtroom's vintage appearance is a facsimile of the historical design; it includes the judge's bench and jury chairs, which are refurbished originals. Entering the room, an eerie silence prevails. Behind the bench, through closed doors, the judge's chambers hold a small antiquated elevator, a secret passage for those judges who presided over past trials and were in fear for their lives. It served as a method of transportation from the third floor to a hidden exit, where the judges could escape the public eye and leave the building safely.

Stairs leading to the clock tower. *Author's collection.*

Stacks and stacks of old court documents and files occupy at least one room adjacent to the county clerk's office. It was here that one of the clerk's office employees began her memorable yet daunting meeting with the courtroom's ghost. She was performing her last task of a very long day and found herself filing documents late into the evening. Alone in the file room, moving along narrow aisles, a feeling of being watched nudged at her. Looking around, she confirmed that she was indeed alone and continued working. After completing her usual routine of closing up the office, this worker exited through the courtroom and was anxious to leave. It was then that she experienced an unwelcome encounter with one ethereal resident. Not only did this invisible visitor reveal himself to her as a tall, shadowy figure, but he made sure to confirm his presence by brushing her as he hurried by.

Presiding below the main floor of the Grand Old Lady is the Courthouse Shops, a collection of unique shops and businesses that occupy the original English basement of the old courthouse. Recently, the John Dillinger Museum, the legacy of the late Joe Pinkston, was added to the exclusive mix. It displays a number of relics and collectibles and is a chronological walk along "the twisted road that led to Dillinger's death."

By preserving the dungeon-like atmosphere, equipped with the original bricks and barred alcoves, it is no wonder that this basement is home to myriad ghosts and paranormal activity. One entity manifests as an apparition of a beautiful lady dressed in clothing indicative of the 1800s. She brings with her the scent of roses and is usually seen strolling up and down the

Lower level of the Lake County Courthouse, the Courthouse Shops. *Author's collection.*

narrow corridor. Yet another occupant of the courthouse basement is observed as a handsome gentleman in a brown suit and fedora. He makes his way from the direction of the men's bathroom toward Heidi's House of Clock Repair, ascending the stairs across from the shop. Curious shopkeeper Jack has followed this ghostly figure, only to witness him dissolving at the top of the stairs. He commented, "There's a ghost, a gentleman, that walks from the men's room up the stairs. He wears a brown coat and some kind of brown pants. We've chased him, and nobody's ever caught him. The stairs are locked; there's nowhere to go. I've seen him twice; the guy from the restaurant has seen him a couple times."

The original brick walls, the only present observer to the courthouse's past, have been known to whisper to visitors as well. They reveal their secrets through echoes of laughter, muffled conversations and footsteps that resound throughout this eclectic collection of shops. Jack has also been witness to disembodied voices heard around the shop where he works and says, "And then there's also been voices. We hear voices in the middle of the night; laughter coming down here. And then one night, the lady was painting in her store, and the radio in the candy shop came on all by itself, and the next morning it was off."

The endeared Crown Point Courthouse will always be infamous for her history and successful struggle to remain one of the finest examples of architectural expression in Indiana. Many will gaze upon her formidable towers and muse about an era gone by. One thing will remain true for sure: the Grand Old Lady is a mysterious old girl that legends and ghost stories are made of.

CHAPTER 2

TOAST THE GHOSTS

SPIRITS OF THE PRIME STEAKHOUSE

It was a stellar evening. The company had been great. In fact, the conversation was flowing. The steak was done to perfection, and a feeling of contentment was gained from a combination of the excellent merlot and slightly warming atmosphere. The lighting was low, and the buzz of the other patrons enjoying their evening was comforting.

Very slowly, a cold sensation found its way to the table, almost like a motionless draft. Then, what followed was an inkling of being watched. All four dinner guests refused to acknowledge the interloper that chose to invade their evening. Eventually, the enormous gold gilded mirror facing the table revealed what each guest had known all along: the ghost of Prime Steakhouse had finally made its appearance!

The historic and diverse Crown Point downtown area offers a wide variety of dining options. Whether the day calls for an amazing sub sandwich to satisfy the need for a quick lunch or the evening beckons to experience an intimate gourmet dinner with good friends, there is no lack of choices found here.

Infamous for offering twenty-day wet-aged steaks and a variety of fresh seafood is the Prime Steakhouse. Guests are pampered by an excellent wait staff and find themselves completely immersed in a Chicago-like atmosphere. Casual dinner or elegant date night, 109 West Joliet Street is the destination to experience both. Upon entering, steep stairs nestled in a narrow hallway lead to Umi Sushi and Lounge, just another exciting venue featuring the freshest and most stunning sushi in the area. If martinis and

Business section of Joliet Street. *Courtesy of Calumet Regional Archives, Indiana University Northwest.*

custom-made cocktails are on the agenda for the evening, Umi Sushi will satisfy the most particular palate. To the right of the entryway, Prime Steakhouse achieves the perfect balance of history and present décor by revealing the original brick walls of the 130-year-old structure.

Although the buildings on the south side of the Square were the first to encircle the Crown Point Courthouse, they still had many years ahead of them to be developed. In 1841, only four years after the log courthouse was constructed to serve the citizens of Crown Point, the town did see rapid improvement. Chimneys made of sticks and clay were being replaced by brick. Physicians and lawyers soon took up residence, and their offices were opened for business. Schools and churches were organized, and buildings for their use were created.

As the needs of the townspeople increased, several entrepreneurs responded, and downtown Crown Point was created. One of the prosperous proprietors was Jacob Young, a talented tinsmith, who purchased the tinware store from William Price. Located at 115 West Joliet Street, just a few doors down from what now is the Prime Steakhouse, this business venture for Jacob would prove to be his last. Tinplate workers were popular in the 1800s for manufacturing and repairing tinware such as pewter. Upon entering his store, one could find an excellent selection of pewter cups, coffeepots, water pitchers, forks, spoons and candle holders. In addition to making and selling his tinware, Jacob made available an array of stoves. He sold a wide variety of parlor stoves, cook stoves and box stoves. Typically cast iron, box stoves had six burners, were fueled by coal or wood and were used primarily for cooking. Parlor stoves and box stoves were used in every room for providing heat, as fireplaces were no longer found to be efficient. Jacob's business prospered for four years. Gradually, those he encountered observed a noticeable change in his personality. He began to show signs of severe depression, smiled less and less and complained of not being able to sleep. A two-day trip with his wife and young son to visit his brother-in-law, C.V. Holton, three miles southeast of Crown Point sealed his fate. He committed suicide in the parlor of Holton's home by shooting himself in the throat. Sometimes the deceased's unsettled spirit can leave an imprint of their moods or characteristics on a particular location. Bad events or situations can always increase the probability of an area, not specific to a particular building, being haunted. Could it be Jacob's presence that diners perceive at 109 West Joliet Street?

In 1865, the population of Crown Point increased dramatically, and as the railroad came to this small town, so did iron rails and telegraph wires, connecting Crown Point with the hustle and bustle of the outside world. The town was incorporated in 1868 and was protected by its own fire department beginning in 1869.

Occupying the intersection of Main and Joliet Streets in the early 1870s were the Miller Hotel and the Heiser Hotel, which offered their hospitality to local residents as well as travelers. The Heiser Hotel was managed by Peter and Margaret Heiser and was one of the "best known hostelries in Lake County." This same corner was home to the Cheshire Hall in 1873, named after its builder, W.W. Cheshire. Built in the Italianate style, which was popular during the 1850s through the 1870s, it featured a flat-topped roof with brackets and decorative window moldings. Two or more stories tall, this type of architecture featured large storefront windows and became the hallmark style of Main Street America.

The current Crown Point Courthouse, constructed with bricks from the Henry Wise Brickyard in Crown Point, became the pride of Lake County and the center of the Crown Point Square in 1878. The south side of the Square began to develop as a commercial district and consisted of Schwartz's Drug Store, Krinbill's dry goods and grocery, Eder Bros. Tobbaconists, Minas Bros. Harness, Ruschli and Simon Meats, Jack Houk Shoes, Strike Conway Shoe Repair, Wise the Tinner and John Prier Agricultural Implements.

Nestled between Krinbill's and Eder Bros. Tobbaconists was Church's Grocery, now the Prime Steakhouse. In 1886, the ground floor of this edifice was a general store supplying local residents with necessities. Crowded along every wall were many shelves displaying coffee beans, spices, oatmeal, flour and sugar. Perishables were also available, such as eggs, milk and cheese. Due to limited space, the floor could be found littered with boxes, barrels, crates and tables holding fruits and vegetables. The front counter held display cases for smaller items like hard candy, cigars and tobacco; a coffee grinder; scales for weighing merchandise; and a cash register. Stored below in the cellar was a surplus of merchandise such as dry goods and cleaning supplies. Above the grocery, on the second floor, an armory stored rifles, pistols and ammunition. The third floor was an empty hall, perhaps used for social gatherings and meetings.

The Grand Old Lady, as the current Crown Point Courthouse is fondly referred to, was to become the center of the Square in 1878. Almost fifteen years later, electric lighting cast its romantic glow along the busy streets of

Crown Point Square around 1900. *Courtesy of Lake County, Indiana Historical Society.*

the Square. By 1892, the second floor of Church's Grocery was occupied by a printing shop, taking advantage of the newly found power source and providing its customers with periodicals, magazines and stationery.

The Chicagoland area in the 1930s was one of the major areas in the United States that was strongly associated with criminal activity. This period of time, called the gangster era, was associated with gangsters, the mafia and speakeasies. Speakeasies were hidden establishments that were created to sell and consume alcoholic beverages during Prohibition. It was illegal to make or sell alcohol in the United States from 1920 to 1933. These speakeasies got their name from a bartender who urged his customers to "speak easy," not drawing any attention to the fact that they were buying or consuming alcohol illegally. Bartenders were usually in cahoots with gangs and members of the establishment to conceal speakeasies by hiding them behind secret walls or creating them underground. Many storefronts appeared as legitimate businesses, only to be known to a few select members as places to obtain alcohol by using a secret knock on a door or uttering a password.

Descending the narrow stairs through a door near the back of 109 West Joliet Street, now Prime Steakhouse, the feeling of claustrophobia is overwhelming. Lighting the vintage passageway are light bulbs that reach eagerly into the darkness below but fail to assure the individual of safe passage. Once down in the basement, surrounding walls of old brick close in to suggest that there is no escaping this vast room. Focusing ahead, a small door beckons to be opened to reveal the secret that has existed for perhaps eighty years. Badly in need of repair, a gap supported by wooden beams and stretching a distance of about twenty feet strongly supports the existence of underground tunnels beneath the streets of the Crown Point Square. One can only speculate if this tunnel was created during Prohibition and was a means of shuttling alcohol or passengers through a discreet underground system.

In 1933, the Twenty-First Amendment to the Constitution was passed and ratified, ending Prohibition. With the legalization of producing and consuming alcohol came the establishment of the American neighborhood tavern. Now, people from all walks of life in the community could come together to share and discuss news and politics.

Offering just that atmosphere, 109 West Joliet Street became Henderlong's Tavern in 1948. Just a few years later, the establishment was sold to Frank Dian, and he made it his own by renaming it Dian's Tap. Some slight remodeling—paneling the walls and dropping the ceiling—made this family-owned establishment a popular place that provided many memories. The second floor offered those interested a competitive game of pool. Arched doorways and dim lighting created an atmosphere that was described as uncomfortable. It was in this area that the ghostly residents of Prime Steakhouse first made their presence known. John, a regular customer of Dian's Tap, recalls, "I used to think that pool room was creepy. And the archways…didn't want to go through them. Yeah, really felt creepy up there." Different people can experience a wide variety of feelings when coming in contact with a spirit. Some people feel goose bumps, some experience an increase in heartbeat and some feel a heavy, dense change in energy.

The local ghost story that is associated with Dian's Tap is a common one in drinking establishments and centers on a frequent customer named William. It was customary for William to spend long hours at the bar, chatting with locals, and he would leave just as the bar was getting ready to close for the night. During one such occasion, as the bartender was cleaning up, he noticed William was still sitting there and needed a nudge to wake him and get him on his way. Unfortunately, sometime during his last visit, unbeknownst to any of the patrons that evening, William had quietly passed away, his head resting on top of the bar. Some say it is William's spirit that remains behind, watching over the customers and joining in the conversation as he enjoyed doing many years ago. Could he be occupying the empty bar stool next to you?

The 1970s saw the closing of Dian's Tap, and the sign outside 109 West Joliet Street was replaced by one that declared Curley's as the drinking establishment within. It was a comfortable workingman's bar during the day and a dance club upstairs at night.

As the Crown Point Square became known as a downtown historic district and the popular destination for entertainment, many entrepreneurs were meeting the needs of the community by providing excellent dining options. Themed restaurants, pizza parlors and nightclubs were met with enthusiastic approval. In 1988, a privately held company listed as Rich Mill, Inc., purchased the building and created an amazing venue called Chicago's, offering a gourmet menu and a downtown Chicago atmosphere.

In an attempt to create this atmosphere, the owner acquired the original bar that was used in the 1933 Chicago World's Fair. Adding to the uniqueness of this vintage bar is the imbedded heel print of the famous 1930s burlesque dancer Sally Rand from her performance at the fair. Born as Hattie Helen Gould Beck on April 3, 1904, Rand was a burlesque dancer and actress noted for her famous "fan dance," where she would adorn her body with "cosmetic whitewash" and powder and then dance behind two large, feathery fans. Concluding her performance by revealing herself, she gave the appearance of a nude alabaster statue when, in fact, she was clothed in a beige body suit. Swooping to the tune of "Clair de Lune," she was deemed the hit of the Midway and, in many respects, the fair itself.

Although Chicago's saw great success for many years, new owners presented the Crown Point Square with a restaurant named Amoré, creating a more romantic and nostalgic establishment. Intimate date nights here began with appetizers such as calamari, stuffed mussels, bruschetta and a wide variety of savory soups and salads served on cloth-clad tables downstairs. Offered on the main menu were Italian dishes, such as pastas, paninis and seafood, prepared exquisitely by head chef Carl Lindskog. Elegant but laid-back, the 109 Lounge upstairs appealed to the late-night crowd by featuring live local bands and thirty-four specialty martinis.

On several nights, after the amps were silenced, some patrons felt an overwhelming sense of sadness descend upon them, despite the vibrant energy the band created during the evening. Feeling emotion without understanding why and empathically picking up on the energy of a spirit that is nearby is common in many locations where a person has experienced strong and sometimes tragic emotions while alive. People who have the ability to sense spirit in this manner are called clairsentient. Clairsentience is the ability to feel and experience the energy in an intuitive way. Was there a melancholy spirit present in the upper level of 109 West Joliet Street that has remained unsettled for over one hundred years? Or could it be a more recent soul who is trying to communicate with anyone who will listen? Do the restless spirits that occupy the space of this century-old building create an unbalanced atmosphere? Are they mindfully driving businesses out?

When Theodoros and Toula Klideris decided to bring their talents as restaurateurs to the city of Crown Point, they knew their success would begin at 109 West Joliet Street. It was the perfect location for Theodoros to fulfill his passion of creating a regal steakhouse in the Crown Point Square. Prime Steakhouse was purchased in January 2013 and presented its grand opening in October of the same year. By converting the two-story stage area to an intimate dining niche, retaining the famous bar from the 1933 Chicago World's Fair and restoring the original brick walls and tin ceiling, Toula mastered the art of creating a classic dining experience.

Was it this final renovation to the building that awakened the ghosts that have dwelled here over the years, or was it the act of love that went into preserving the historical interior? Sometimes, by remodeling, and therefore

Prime Steakhouse. *Author's collection.*

changing the environment, a restless soul can become uncomfortable with the outcome. Ghosts that have grown so accustomed to their usual surroundings go into a kind of sleep, and sudden changes to their environment can spark paranormal activity. On the other hand, many spirits that are stirred because of a noisy renovation simply want to say "I'm still here." For whatever reason, the employees as well as the patrons of Prime Steakhouse are forced to share space with a variety of past souls that have chosen to remain here.

"Mirror, mirror, on the wall, who is that I see, passing by thee?" Taking up nearly the entire wall, the impressive mirror near the back of the restaurant is said to reflect more than just diners. Witnessed by waiters as well as dinner guests is the shimmering form of a young man with long, dark hair and a knee-length jacket. Fondly referred to as "Steve," he appears as either a fleeting glimpse passing in front of the mirror or a shadowy figure standing off in a corner. Offering no interaction, Steve seems satisfied with making a brief appearance and then vanishes very quickly. The steakhouse staff has the opinion that he depicts someone from the 1970s, but he could just as likely be a gentleman from the early 1890s, when this structure was built. Given the melancholy atmosphere of the upstairs room, one could even go so far as to suppose that this could be the spirit of Jacob Young, the depressed tinsmith who occupied the building just a few doors down. Is Jacob's spirit lost and wandering the area he was once so familiar with?

In addition to the wandering male spirit, Prime Steakhouse guests experience a number of paranormal phenomena while on the premises. Lights above the bars both upstairs and downstairs blink on and off during the course of any evening. Shadow people are observed lurking in low-lighted areas throughout the restaurant. Shadow people are usually seen out of the corner of one's eye, having a dark, human shape. Because they are dark, the details of their appearance are lacking.

Original wooden stairs, set in a narrow passageway, lead to Umi Sushi, the world-class sushi venue above. Do not be surprised if this short walk up twenty-two stairs produces chills and an uncomfortably anxious feeling. Proceeding to the back alcove where the restrooms are located also proves to be quite an experience for those who are sensitive to spiritual energy. Physical conditions, such as sudden dizziness and nausea, are common while standing in the century-old corridor. In theory, spirits are pure electromagnetic energy, and electromagnetic fields can affect the body. Depending on how sensitive the person is to EM emissions, symptoms can include irritability, headaches and nausea.

Keeping the lights functioning in one of the two restrooms is a constant challenge for the present managers of Prime Steakhouse due to the fact that they pop and explode on a regular basis. Sometimes, spirits draw energy from a light bulb by simply overpowering the fragile structure of the light bulb's light mechanism. The least power source can blow a light bulb.

Nevertheless, each night a quiet calm descends on 109 West Joliet Street. The lights are dimmed and the doors are locked for the night. The closing crew begins their task of clearing the tables, washing the glasses and preparing the restaurant for yet another day. Everyone here is familiar with the spirits that claim Prime Steakhouse as their earthly home. They believe the veil that separates the living and the dead is thin and welcome the spirits with open arms.

Prime Steakhouse is an enticing destination for those in the mood for an expertly prepared meal and historic atmosphere. Visitors are not afraid to sit at the bar, have a cocktail and put their fingers in the famous heel print of Sally Rand. If the lights go out and the barstool next to them moves ever so slightly, they just assume it's William sharing a "spirit" with them, and they toast the ghost!

CHAPTER 3

THE GRAY LADY OF CARNEGIE LIBRARY

For the citizens of Crown Point more than one hundred years ago, the building at 223 South Main Street was the proud accomplishment that served the community as its first library. Now, over a century later, it is remembered as the source of one of the town's most famous ghost stories.

In 1857, twenty years before the historical Crown Point Courthouse was built, the citizens of this growing community created a lending library system. It was established by the McClure Library Association, a common idea founded by Benjamin Franklin in the early 1700s. After the establishment of the location at 106 South Main Street, members of this book club would pay a small fee to join and bring books to a meeting room, where other members could benefit from borrowing and returning them. Before long, the membership accepted donations to purchase new books to increase the library's collection. Unfortunately, by 1885, the McClure Library Association had closed, transferring the 148 volumes the association had acquired to a local public school and resulting in the disuse of the collection for twenty years.

Young America found itself engrossed in an easily attainable source of entertainment provided by books from some of the leading authors of the nineteenth century. From depicting the risqué and romantic tale of Hester Prynne in *The Scarlet Letter*, by Nathaniel Hawthorne, to disclosing the tribulations suffered by the slaves in *Uncle Tom's Cabin*, by Harriet Beecher Stowe, American literature was gaining popularity.

As the demand for modern reading material increased, a nine-member board formed in 1906 to begin the process of giving Crown Point sufficient space for a library. The board purchased the O.G. Wheeler property, one block from the Square, and began construction at 223 South Main Street. With a donation of $12,000 from Andrew Carnegie, an industrialist turned philanthropist, in addition to local contributions, the building was completed for $35,000.

Most of the libraries built by Andrew Carnegie were unique and adopted several styles of architecture. The style of the building was usually chosen by the community; however, there were guidelines to be followed. Each structure was similar in the simple but formal style and welcomed patrons through a prominent doorway. Carnegie also encouraged the entrance of the library to be accessible only by stairs, for he believed it was a symbol of elevation by learning. A lamppost at the entryway was also encouraged to symbolize "enlightenment."

The citizens of Crown Point adopted the Classical Revival style of architecture, popular from 1895 to 1950. Utilizing red brick, this style was inspired by the World's Columbian Exposition in Chicago held in 1893. Massive columns flanked the impressive portico above a steep climb to the

Carnegie Library. *Author's collection.*

Andrew Carnegie.

front door. Crown Point's new library was clearly going to stand up and be noticed.

The Carnegie Library was dedicated in 1908 and named after its benefactor, Andrew Carnegie. Carnegie, who was born on November 25, 1835, in Dunfermline, Scotland, is considered one of the wealthiest businessmen of the nineteenth century. After making the United States his home, he was employed by the Pennsylvania Railroad and eventually acquired the position of assistant to Thomas Scott, one of the railroad's top officials. Climbing the corporate ladder, Carnegie was promoted to superintendent only three years later and achieved the beginnings of his financial success by investing in the oil business. He left the railroad in 1865 and was employed by the Keystone Bridge Company, focusing his attention on the steel industry.

Andrew Carnegie revolutionized steel production by using technology and methods to manufacture steel more easily, and by 1889, the Carnegie Steel Corporation was one of the largest of its kind in the world. In 1901, Andrew relinquished his involvement in the steel industry, sold his company to the infamous J.P. Morgan for $480 million and began a new chapter in his life.

Carnegie's love of reading inspired him to use his assets to enlighten millions of patrons by building dozens of libraries all over the country. He donated approximately $5 million to the New York Public Library in 1901 so it could expand and build several branches. His dedication to encourage learning led him to establish several trusts or institutions bearing his name, including the Carnegie Institute of Technology in Pittsburgh, Pennsylvania, which is now known as Carnegie-Mellon University. Within ten years, Andrew Carnegie created the Carnegie Foundation for the Advancement of Teaching, the Carnegie Trust for the Universities of Scotland, Carnegie Institute for Science and the Carnegie Endowment for International Peace.

Known as the "patron saint of libraries," Carnegie's prime example of his philanthropy was his construction of 2,509 libraries in the late nineteenth and early twentieth centuries, to an amount of over $55 million. Under segregation, black people were generally denied access to public libraries in the southern United States. Rather than insisting on his libraries being racially integrated, Carnegie funded separate libraries for African Americans. He was responsible for building nine libraries in Lake County and two libraries in Porter County, Indiana. At the time of his death in August 1919, Andrew Carnegie still possessed a fortune of $30 million, which went to the Carnegie Corporation of New York.

In 1906, three groups of board members were chosen to serve the new library in Crown Point. The judge of Lake County appointed Mr. B.F. Hayes as treasurer and Dr. C.J. Tinkham and Mrs. Margaret Pettibone as board members. The town board appointed Mr. John Brown as president and Mrs. J.R.S. Lenney as secretary. To further complete the board selections, the school board appointed Mr. F.F. Heighway as vice president and Mrs. W.A. Scheddell to the board. The honor of the position as the first librarian was given to Marie Hansen of Hammond, Indiana, who years later would have the Hansen Library Branch in Hammond named after her.

In anticipation of the opening of Carnegie Library, 1,500 volumes of reference and nonfiction material from the initial collection of the McClure Library Association were transferred to several new bookshelves. Local residents also contributed to the library's book inventory by donating over $100. The design of Andrew Carnegie's libraries encouraged patrons to browse book collections by displaying them in open stacks. One could choose a particular book on his own and then ask the librarian for assistance.

John Brown, president of the Businessmen's Association. *Courtesy of Lake County, Indiana Historical Society.*

The number of families making Crown Point their home was increasing rapidly. Almost nine hundred new citizens occupied the homes, shopped the Square and attended church in the "Hub of Lake County" by 1913, and naturally many of them were children. Public schools were becoming more numerous, and by 1920, state laws set requirements for children ages eight to fourteen to attend for part of the year. By the turn of the century, school libraries were few and informal. However, in 1901, the Section for Library Work with Children was established, causing government authorities to become more involved. In 1914, the School Libraries section of the American Library Association was appointed and later became known as the American Association for School Libraries.

Children around the country were developing a love for reading, becoming fans of such literary classics as *The Wonderful Wizard of Oz*, written by L. Frank Baum, considered by many to be the great American fairy tale. *Peter Pan*, written by J.M. Barrie, transported America's youth to Neverland and was considered his best work. In 1911, *The Secret Garden*, written by Frances Hodgson Burnett, was published in its entirety; it is now one of her most popular novels.

It was time to designate a space at the Carnegie Library primarily for children, to include these famous classics and make them readily available for everyone. The library board voted unanimously to undertake this project, and in 1914, the South Room of the building was converted to a children's section. The reference volumes were relocated in the back of the library, proving to be a wise decision.

Perhaps it was the remodeling of the library that prompted the appearance of a ghostly apparition, fondly referred to as the "Gray Lady." Renovations can sometimes cause spirits to awake, making an appearance after many years of remaining asleep. They may become uncomfortable when the environment they are accustomed to has changed. The specter first appeared as a tall, human-shaped shadow figure lurking behind the bookshelves in the North Room of the library. Both employees and patrons had reported observing a misty figure standing among the books on several occasions. Stories about this unidentified, mysterious figure began to circulate around the community and soon became local folklore. It was not until photographs of the North and South Rooms of Carnegie Library were taken and a ghostly silhouette appeared in one of the photos that the sighting was taken seriously. People who viewed the famous photograph believed it revealed the filmy shape of a man who had died several months prior to when the picture was taken. However, others who viewed the photograph claimed it depicted the spirit of the Gray Lady. Either way, it looked like the Carnegie Library had captured its ghost!

The Great Depression, which took place from 1929 to 1939, was the longest-lasting economic tragedy in the Western industrialized world, causing mass unemployment and wiping out millions of United States citizens' bank accounts. It also greatly affected the libraries across the nation by reducing annual tax receipts, which lasted until 1950. Only 765 libraries survived the period between 1930 and 1940. Fortunately, the Carnegie Library in Crown

Point made necessary budget adjustments by reducing collections, supplies and, lastly, personnel.

Crown Point experienced a significant increase in the population from 1950 to 1960. Over 2,500 new citizens elected to make it their home. Now it was time to expand the Carnegie Library to meet the needs of a rapidly growing community. In 1962, the board established a Cumulative Building Fund in anticipation of a much-needed addition to the library. After taking a census of the community, a consultant was employed to make recommendations to utilize the funds in the best manner. It was decided to retain the current Carnegie Library and expand the facility to the rear of the property on South Court Street. In 1971, the library purchased the house located at 214 South Court Street, which was owned by E.T. Brown of the First Presbyterian Church and was originally built by Johnson Wheeler, father of Colonel Wheeler.

An expansion and new building with an entrance on South Court Street was underway. The groundbreaking for the new library took place in late November 1971, and on January 14, 1972, six hundred guests attended its official dedication ceremony. The new extension had a 50,000-volume capacity and a contemporary look and feel. Green walls, orange shelving and rust-colored carpeting greeted the patrons of Carnegie Library, along with over 300,000 books that were transported to the new building.

Containing information on the state of Indiana and Lake County, the Indiana Room was created and included in the new library. Holding books, historical photographs, genealogies, maps and old directories from Crown Point, these numerous resources were made available to researchers in one location. The Indiana Room was dedicated to Joseph E. Brown, board member from 1926 to 1972, and his wife, Avis Brown.

Restoring the Carnegie Library to its magnificence and utilizing it once again for the needs of the community became a priority for the Library Board. Renovations to the original Carnegie Library began in 1973, and the spirit activity began again. In addition to the witnessing of the shadowy image, books began falling off shelves while employees and library patrons watched in amazement.

The Carnegie Center opened to the public in 1974, elegantly equipped to host community meetings and events. The response to the reinvented Carnegie Library was so positive that it became a popular place to hold piano recitals, receptions and even weddings.

The 1980s brought many innovations to the Carnegie Library's modern addition in 1972. On August 11, 1982, the library was officially renamed

Crown Point Community Library. The Reference Department was reconstructed and enlarged, an audiovisual department was added and computer stations kept the adults, students and children of Crown Point up to date on the latest technology.

Adapting the motto "Turning a new leaf…renovating for our future," another renovation to the library was undertaken in 1997. Crown Point Community Library made room for an increase in materials by adding more shelving and adapting to new technology. Replacing the 1970s décor was an updated design that included further seating and designated space for more computers.

A series of paranormal occurrences at the library in 2009 rekindled interest in the Crown Point Community Library's ghost. A local team of four paranormal investigators was invited to explore the interior of the library to gather evidence of reported paranormal activity. Two of the team members began their night searching for ghostly activity in the Indiana Room. While in the back right corner, they recorded a disembodied voice during an EVP (electronic voice phenomenon) session, although the audio was not clear as to what was said. Later, the pair witnessed a bright light slowly passing by the doorway of the room.

The children's corner revealed spirit activity as well. A lady's voice and incessant whispering were evident on walkie-talkie equipment used among the investigators. Could they be experiencing the residual energy of a children's story time session from the past?

Making sure the ghost hunters were not disappointed in their quest to discover evidence of the Carnegie ghost, the unearthly residents obliged by using their energy to drain batteries, produce knocking noises and cause books to fall.

After forty years of serving the community, the Crown Point Community Library closed on September 29, 2012. Construction on a new, modern structure was underway. The Carnegie Center on Main Street remained a historical structure for nearly two years. Although it would serve to be temporary, the ghosts of Carnegie Library were happily returned to a time when they were free to exist, undisturbed in their supernatural world.

In 2014, law books replaced the hundreds of library books that had occupied the building known as the Carnegie Library. Attorney Michael Lambert decided to purchase the building and moved his law offices there, due to its ideal location and historical significance. The doorway connecting the Carnegie building to the annex on South Court Street was forever sealed, allowing the sale of the annex to an interested buyer.

The new three-story Crown Point Community Library, located on North Main Street, welcomed its first patrons in October 2012. Readers stepped into the future with a first-floor Internet café, beautifully landscaped outdoor seating area and over forty-six thousand square feet of space to serve Lake County. Making readily available resources about the local history of Crown Point, the Indiana Room was constructed on the second floor, including a display case of photographs from the original Carnegie Library. It may have been the photograph taken in the North Room, revealing the image of a spirit, or perhaps the relocation of a favorite book that invited the return of the Gray Lady.

The first reports of strange occurrences came from librarians left alone in the eerie quiet of the library. After closing hours, while performing the task of returning books to the shelves, they observed from across the room several books dropping from the shelves onto the floor. Stories of seeing the gray apparition of a lady, dressed in old clothing and peering out from behind the bookshelves, resurfaced. Patrons also avoided certain areas of the library where they felt they were being watched.

For over one hundred years the Gray Lady of Carnegie Library has been a favorite legend of the citizens of Crown Point. Most libraries are deemed haunted due to the possibility of former librarians remaining behind to mind the books or the spirits of loyal patrons who cannot seem to leave their favorite reading place. Perhaps the ghost that inhabits the Crown Point library received her name from the famous Gray Lady of Willard Library. The Willard Library, located about three hundred miles from Crown Point, in Evansville, Indiana, was built in the Victorian Gothic design in 1885. The apparition of the Gray Lady of Willard Library has been sighted continually since the 1930s and has been described as a lady dressed in gray, 1800s-style clothing: a long gray dress, high-topped shoes, a gray hat and veil or just a shawl. She has made numerous appearances to librarians and patrons alike and has been captured on film, as well as video. In addition to turning water on and off in the library, she moves objects and leaves behind the heavy scent of her perfume. One theory on the identity of the Gray Lady of Willard Library is that it may be Louise, the daughter of Willard Carpenter, one of Evansville's influential pioneers, who built the library.

As for the legend of the Gray Lady of Carnegie Library, it continues as one of the many beloved stories of Crown Point. One is bound to spot her in the Crown Point Community Library, either discreetly keeping watch over the books or making an appearance in her famed photo.

CHAPTER 4

OLD TOWN SQUARE ANTIQUES

There are a great number of people who are drawn to the experiences of the past. Some thirst for knowledge and research past lifetimes or events to share facts and information with the public. Others seek a variety of items to acquire while organizing, categorizing and displaying them for profit or pleasure. However, there are still others whose souls are simply connected to the past. A book once held by a student from decades gone by, an empty perfume bottle that suggests just a hint of floral scent, a paperweight that once secured valuable documents on an heirloom desk or a mixing bowl that created hundreds of cookies in a kitchen from the 1950s are just a few finds that can almost transport one back in time.

For this population, there are antique shops. Here, one can browse among as few as one hundred or as many as one thousand items that are labeled antique, vintage or collectible. To be considered an antique, an item must be at least fifty years old, although many experts deem a true antique to be at least one hundred years of age. Antique items are valued for their historic significance. Collectibles fall into the fifty-years-old category and are often more attainable for the average shopper. The term "vintage" describes items that are recycled back into fashion and are twenty-five years old or less.

Believers in the supernatural strongly contend that lost souls can take up residence in objects and continue to interact with an object long after they are gone. Most common are personal objects that were handled often by the owner or meant something special to them while they were alive. Jewelry, combs, hair receivers, perfume bottles, compacts, keys, purses, wallets and clothing are among these personal belongings that are most likely to contain the past owner's energetic imprint. These items, when held or displayed, can make one who is sensitive to spiritual activity feel cold, anxious, sad, happy or even angry. The psychic talent associated with reading the energy remaining in objects is call psychometry. Dolls, antique headboards or bedframes, paintings such as self-portraits and evening gowns have been found to hold the most spiritual energy. Previously owned items can even give off a particular smell or cause one to experience a flash of a particular memory or event that was important in the past owner's life. Severe hauntings of extremely personal items can even cause frequent nightmares, bring bad luck and cause frequent illness.

What could one expect if thousands of antique, vintage or collectible items were displayed in one place for the public to browse and perhaps purchase? Would this plethora of bygone treasures create an atmosphere perfect for a haunting? Many people associated with the supernatural say yes. Having so many items from the past that could be absorbed by residual energy could result in a display of ghostly activity.

One such antique shop where this scenario holds true is the Antique Mall at 101–7 West Joliet Street. Situated on the corner of Main Street and West Joliet Street in the historic Crown Point Square, this building is proud to bear the year 1873. Providing the Crown Point Square with treasures of the past, the history of its contents is no match for the history that is assimilated in its walls.

Well before the Crown Point Courthouse took up its residence as the center of the town square, W.W. Cheshire was a prominent figure in the blooming town of Crown Point. Arriving from the South during the Civil War, he was appointed superintendent of the Crown Point schools. Recognizing the town's need for a grand and public building where the growing population of Crown Point could gather for social events, he commissioned the erection of the building at 101 West Joliet Street.

The tall and narrow three-bay, three-story brick building is considered a good example of the Italianate style. Its tall and narrow windows on the second and third floors have segmental arches, ornate limestone window hoods and limestone sills. The first floor contained an enormous room equipped with every convenience of its time. The building was dedicated to the town in 1873 and was named after its owner and builder, W.W. Cheshire. Crown Point had acquired its town hall, where lectures, concerts, dramas and social events would be held with the utmost elegance.

Men could be observed arriving in top hats and long coats as they escorted their ladies attired in long, corset-like dresses, bustled and flowing. Evening lectures and political speeches were given by the finest of speakers and attended by the local residents of Crown Point, as well as those who dwelled in Lake County. Cheshire Hall became known as the "abode of journalism" soon after it opened its doors to an eager public. The most notable lectures were given under the auspices of the Lecture Club, of which Mrs. J.W. Youche was secretary. Some of these famous speakers were Professor David Swing, a teacher and clergyman who was the most popular Chicago preacher of his time, and William McKendree Carleton, an American poet who wrote about his rural life in Lenawee County, Hudson, Michigan. At only twenty-five years old, Carleton wrote poems that captured national attention and catapulted him into literary prominence, and he lectured from coast to coast for the rest of his life. The lecture podium was also host to Reverend James K. Applebee, a notable Shakespearean scholar who recited and discussed the sonnets of Shakespeare, *Macbeth* and *Romeo and Juliet*. Home talent making an enjoyable appearance included Reverend Timothy Ball and Judge Field.

One of the most notable speakers appearing at Cheshire Hall was Susan B. Anthony. Her fight for women's rights in the 1800s, along with Elizabeth Cady Stanton, was responsible for the Nineteenth Amendment to the United States Constitution, giving women the right to vote in 1920. It was from the second floor of the Cheshire Hall that Anthony's booming voice could be heard as she gave her iconic speech "Women's Rights to the Suffrage":

> *The only question left to be settled now is: Are women persons? And I hardly believe any of our opponents will have the hardihood to say they are not. Being persons, then, women are citizens; and no State has a right to make any law, or to enforce any old law, that shall abridge their privileges or immunities. Hence, every discrimination against women in the constitutions and laws of the several States is today null and void, precisely as in every one against Negroes.*

On one morning four years ago, Dee, an employee who is an antique vendor as well at the Antique Mall, was setting up her booth, number 106, when she witnessed the apparition of a lady. She said:

> *I moved in here four years ago; my husband and my brother were helping me move. We saw a lady. She was like…in black-and-white, like no color at all, so we called her the Gray Lady, and we saw her about three times just*

during the process of moving in. She did walk through my booth and in the kitchen where the hat lady is. This lady did have a hat on and stockings and old-fashioned shoes. I never heard her speak, and I have not seen her since.

Could this "Gray Lady" be the formidable spirit of Susan B. Anthony, strolling through the area while admiring the items that Dee was displaying and perhaps doing some shopping?

The Cheshire Hall was also host to social events for the young citizens of Crown Point. Young ladies who were eligible to marry attended dances on the upper floors to socialize with eligible bachelors. Banjos, violins and guitars could be heard across the Square as the couples circled, promenaded and waltzed to popular tunes of that day.

The next thirty years brought many changes to the town of Crown Point, as residents welcomed progress. Electric lights brightened the new wooden sidewalks, made from the finest pine lumber, to make evening outings around the Square more enjoyable. In 1891, Chicagoan Arthur

Crown Point Square, early 1800s.

B. Cotton was responsible for the erection of the towering poles and connecting wires that would illuminate the major corners and crosswalks around the Square. Ten arc lights, supplying two thousand candle power each, set the night aglow.

Formation of the Crown Point Telephone Company in 1896 made life even more fulfilling by making communication effortless and satisfying. Owner Martin Rudolph directed the installation of black and white painted poles, twenty-five feet from the ground, that would support telephone wires. The first telephone was installed in the water pumping station, to be followed by residential service. For $1.50 per month, each household could enjoy communication at its fingertips, and businesses could increase their efficiency for just $0.50 more. The first manual switchboard was located above Miller's Grocers on the north side of the Square; in 1923, it was relocated to the second floor of the building previously known as Cheshire Hall.

The manual switchboard was manned by at least eight switchboard operators connecting the phone calls by inserting a pair of phone plugs into the appropriate jacks. Each jack had a light above it that lit up when the telephone receiver was lifted. Callers spoke to the operators at a central office, who then connected a cord to the proper circuit in order to complete the call. Being employed as a telephone operator was serious business, and a supervisor was always present to ensure the operators were quiet and efficient. The telephone operators had to sit with perfect posture for long hours in straight-backed chairs and were not permitted to communicate with one another.

The Cheshire Hall also became the home of the National Tea Company in the early 1940s. National Tea grocery stores were the largest retail chain of grocery stores in the 1920s and remained among the ten largest grocery chains in the United States for most of the twentieth century. Although butcher shops and fresh produce stands were still popular, the grocery store in the 1940s brought fresh meat, fresh produce and dry goods together under one roof, to make the concept of one-stop shopping convenient.

In the 1940s, 1950s and 1960s, Cheshire Hall welcomed the occupants of Crown Point once again. Instead of coming to the Cheshire Hall for lectures and quiet conversations, young men gathered downstairs for other reasons. Echoing through the building were the sounds of laughter and the loud crack of billiard balls. Ferrero's was no place for ladies, as men socialized while smoking cigarettes and cigars and engaging in a competitive game of pool.

Crown Point Telephone Company switchboard operators.

Below the pool hall, in the basement, men could get a haircut by the barber known as Snowball. Snowball was quite a character and was well known for the array of old Crown Point photos displayed on the walls of his shop. The shop was a memorable gathering place where gentlemen spent time sharing stories while getting groomed to look their best.

On the east side of the building, a narrow staircase led the way to a taxi company, also located in the basement of 101 Joliet Street. Here, individuals hired transportation for destinations in and near the town of Crown Point.

Aria, one of the long-residing managers at the Antique Mall, has heard innumerable stories relating to spirit activity in the mall's basement. Vendors and visitors to the mall have told her that "the basement is loaded with spirits." It is extremely common for one to discover cold spots among the numerous items of furniture and vintage memorabilia in the lowest level of the building. One of the most reported areas of frigid temperatures is the stairs going up from the basement level to the second floor. Cold spots are areas of localized coldness or sudden decrease in ambient temperature, leaving individuals with supernatural chills. The common belief is that in order to manifest, ghosts must pull energy in the form of heat from the environment.

Five-and-dime variety stores began to find their way into local communities in the 1960s, and soon the Ben Franklin variety store replaced the billiard room at Cheshire Hall. Here, children browsed the aisles for paper dolls, playing cards, jigsaw puzzles and coloring books. As the items were inexpensive, many an allowance was spent at Ben Franklin. Moms and dads have fond memories of purchases like costume jewelry and fishing bobbers. The transition of small variety stores to larger department stores of the 1970s—such as Shopper's World, Topps, Zayre and Venture—eventually led to the closing of these stores, and Ben Franklin was no exception.

Nino and Guiseppina Bruscemi, the owners of the Cheshire Hall in 1976, embarked on their own entrepreneurship by opening an Italian restaurant in the 109-year-old hall in 1979. The establishment highlighted home-style cooking by offering menu items such as a variety of veal dishes, chicken cacciatore, spaghetti, linguini with clam sauce, fish and squid. Many renovations were made to the building to depict an Italianate style. Renovations to buildings are often speculated to be the cause of spirit activity. Undetectable spirits that are comfortable in their surroundings can be awakened by changes in the environment that they are accustomed to. Considering the number of times this building has been renovated, it's not surprising that it is extremely haunted.

The Cheshire Hall was bestowed a favor in 1987 when the Old Town Square Antique Mall took up residence within its historic walls and, in some ways, returned it to the nineteenth century. Three floors of 101 West Joliet Street were once again adorned with delicately designed brooches, elegant hats, compacts and lipstick cases from an era gone by. As one makes their

Cheshire Hall as Ben Franklin, 1964.

way through the numerous displays of items from decades ago, it is easy to become immersed in the past and forget the year is 2017. Perhaps that is the case for the countless souls who remain there and feel compelled to make their presence known.

Rita, who has been an employee as well as a dealer at the antique mall for almost thirty years, has been aware of its ghostly occupants ever since she unlocked its doors. Soon after the mall opened, a quaint Russian tearoom on the third floor offered guests a comfortable place to sit and chat while enjoying a cup of specialty tea and scrumptious sweets. It was here that Rita recalls her first experience as a server in the tearoom. The window held a separate air-conditioning unit that operated by turning a button on and off. It was the opening employee's decision when to turn the unit on, depending on the temperature of the room. Rita remembers the unit turning on and off by itself constantly and the room being freezing cold, even when the air conditioner was not operating. Often, when Rita would enter the restaurant's kitchen area, all of the electrical appliances would be unplugged. One morning, as Rita was readying the seating area of the tearoom, the owner was in the kitchen. She called for Rita to witness yet another extraordinary happening. When Rita joined her co-worker in the kitchen, she asked out loud, "Is there a ghost in here?" and all at once, the napkins that were kept on the top shelf came flying out at them and scattered all over the floor. This is a classic example of an intelligent haunting, due to the fact that the spirit is aware of its surroundings and is able to interact and communicate with the living.

The three women who manage the antique mall get constant reports of supernatural activity from shop vendors and visitors. A frequent guest to the mall has witnessed an apparition of a woman in one of the rocking chairs in a back booth on the second floor. She has seen her on more than one occasion and actually thought she was one of the dealers there.

On another occasion, one of the shop's booth owners decided to bring her mother, who was a retired schoolteacher, along with her to the mall. It was after closing hours, and the vendor thought it would be nice to have some company as she was rearranging and adding to her displayed items. The lights were low, and the shop was eerily quiet. After several minutes, her mother turned to her and asked if she could hear the children laughing and running up and down the aisles. She told her mother that she couldn't possibly have heard anyone, because they were all alone in the building.

Could the children's energy still be present among the rows of old trinkets and toys from the five-and-dime? Perhaps the retired schoolteacher experienced an instance of a residual haunting. She may have been more open to the sounds of the children because of her close relationships with children over the years. The strong, happy emotions hundreds of children experienced during the time 101 West Joliet Street was the five-and-dime could be the reason the residual energy of the children remains. The events that took place many years ago in this building could have left an imprint on the atmosphere that was merely being "played back" like a tape.

Whether the Old Town Square Antique Mall harbors ghosts due to its prominent exhibition of antiquities or its obvious ties with the past is no matter. What holds true in this notable building is the nostalgic emotion that is evoked in the casual shopper or devoted collector. The feeling one experiences is most often one of contentment and fond memories of days gone by, although the mall does have its share of shadowy corners and dark sentiments. Choose wisely when deciding to take a previously owned item home. The artfully crafted mirror that has now found its place above the dressing table might just reflect an image that is not one's own!

CHAPTER 5

GYPSY'S GRAVEYARD

CURSE OF THE GYPSIES

Everyone loves a good ghost story. Not every ghost story is told in a hushed voice around a dwindling campfire, causing those believers and skeptics to look behind them. More often than not, a good tale of the supernatural comes from a friend or neighbor across a kitchen table or over a cup of coffee. These stories usually relate to a ghostly occurrence someone has experienced in the house he just bought or a place he recently visited. Some ghost stories are recited early in adolescence and involve the "haunted house" down the block, causing one to go the long way home to avoid passing it at any cost. The story of Gypsy's Graveyard is none of these. The tale of this solemn and eerie cemetery is a legend. A legend is a partially true story based on some fact or element of truth that is passed on from generation to generation and reflects the beliefs of the culture from which it originates.

Gypsy's Graveyard is located on the outskirts of Crown Point, where 155th Street and South Grove Road have reserved a place for those who have left the land of the living. Renamed Southeast Grove Cemetery, it often goes unnoticed by motorists focused on their destination, oblivious to the small gated community that is now "home" to those who were once among the living. Anonymous, this modest graveyard displays no sign that confirms its identity. Towering trees that come together on each side of this two-lane road, like hands folded in solemn prayer, ban any sunlight from filtering through. Across the street, prestigious homes, set far back, most with iron gates and long driveways, attempt to remain hidden. Glancing into Southeast Grove Cemetery, over its shabby chain-link fence, a sense of peaceful normalcy

Southeast Grove Cemetery (Gypsy's Graveyard). *Author's collection.*

prevails. Narrow rows of gravestones, their engravings worn by time and weather, beckon to be read. The names of the souls who rest here and the dates that reflect when they lived their lives are sometimes barely legible. Despite the poor condition of a number of headstones, they successfully reveal the lives that began and ended in the early 1800s. Intermingled with these 150-year-old markers are more modern tributes to loved ones. The most recent burial here was in 2012, and the "vacancy" sign is still glowing for this eternal hotel. The usual monuments and markers, flowers and vigils occupy the grounds, but it is toward the back of the cemetery, where birch and oak trees reach their greedy branches to the far boundaries of the graveyard, that the legend began more than a century ago.

In 1837, Eagle Creek Township occupied the southeastern corner of Lake County, its southern half being located in the Kankakee region. It consisted mainly of high prairie pleasant groves in the north, and islands, marshes and swamps in the south. This southern half became known as Southeast Grove. Of all the groves in Lake County, it was the largest and was circular in shape. Early writers referred to it as "the finest," as it was overwhelmed with oak and hickory trees. Some of the earliest settlers include the Flint family, George Parkinson, Orlando V. Servis and Orrin Smith, who came between 1836 and 1837. Alexander F. Brown brought his family along with hired men from Schenectady County, New York, to embark on a new journey in 1840. He secured land from the government and farmed successfully in this region until 1849, when he was thrown from his wagon and died one week later. Besides being among the first settlers of this area, he is also recognized as one of the leading and most influential residents of this county by being responsible for his honest convictions and in shaping public policy. In 1884, his son, John Brown, was the prominent figure in bringing steam dredges and other modern appliances to drain the southern half of the township on a large scale. This beautiful landscape was an open invitation to those settlers whose desire it was to farm the land and raise livestock in its most productive soil. Through John's efforts, this region became noted for its agricultural richness.

The first school was organized by Orlando V. Servis out of his own log cabin around 1843. It also served as a church, Sunday school and the community center for the surrounding area. Although Southeast Grove and Crown Point's population would increase in the next twenty years, at this time, only eight houses and a school building had been built between the Crown Point Square and the far side of Southeast Grove, where seven more families lived.

According to the legend, during the mid-1800s, as the meager population was growing, a band of gypsies was traveling through Southeast Grove, on their way to destinations unknown. The term "gypsy" is a mildly derogatory term that is given to people belonging to the ethnic group known as Rom or Romani. It is a holdover term from when it was thought that these people originated in Egypt. It has now been determined that the Rom migrated to Europe from India about 1,500 years ago. The Romani groups were widely discriminated against because of their dark skin and mysterious culture. They were believed to be outsiders and wanderers who moved from town to town and were rarely accepted in the community. Superstitions concerning gypsies and their link with the supernatural have existed for centuries. Aiding this belief, the gypsies entertained those seeking answers about the future by reading palms and telling fortunes. Myths surrounding gypsies casting curses and hexes are still believed to be true today.

Traveling in decorated wagons, the gypsies set up their campsite in Southeast Grove and began selling hand-crafted jewelry, as well as other wares. Festive music could be heard well into the night, as the gypsy families danced and celebrated their prospective fortune in Southeast Grove. They drew the attention of this small community, and their presence was not welcomed. The gypsies originally planned on staying within the town for about two weeks, but that plan soon came to an end when the townspeople decided to pay them a very unfriendly visit. The farmers and ranchers accused the nomads of stealing their livestock and conducting pagan rituals. They expressed their dislike of the gypsy families by threatening to harm them if they did not pack up and move along in a couple of days.

A number of the gypsies were believed to be afflicted with influenza. More likely, it was the cholera virus. The second cholera pandemic historically took place from 1829 to 1849. Reaching from India across western Asia to Europe, Great Britain and the Americas, as well as east to China and Japan, cholera caused more deaths more quickly than any other epidemic disease in the nineteenth century. It spread rapidly due to the poor quality of the water supply and lack of sanitation. Cholera seemed to afflict its victims instantly. One could awaken healthy and suddenly become violently ill. Suffering from severe dehydration, a person with cholera could die within hours. It is no wonder the gypsies, faced with this devastating illness, asked the townspeople for medical attention and then remained in the camp a few more days until their sick family members felt well enough to travel.

The posse of townsmen showed no mercy to the ailing gypsies and again threatened to harm them if they did not evacuate Southeast Grove the next day. Unfortunately, several members of the gypsy camp died that very night. Fearing for their safety and left with no other option, the gypsies were forced to bury their dead in the very ground on which they had once sang, danced and enjoyed living. Leaving by daybreak, the gypsies left their departed loved ones in mounds of Indiana soil and cursed Southeast Grove vehemently, casting a spell on the town.

Following the gypsies' departure, two of the men who had insisted they leave returned to the gypsy campsite. Amid the smoldering campfires, they found several freshly dug graves. Satisfied that the gypsies had left, they returned home, only to discover a sticky red substance on the bottoms of their shoes and pant legs. The men suddenly believed in the gypsies' curse: it was the blood of the dead gypsies! Rumors that evil and bad luck would befall Southeast Grove spread immediately through the town and have lasted for over 150 years.

For the early pioneers who chose to settle in southern Lake County, it was customary for them to bury the members of their family in small plots near their homes. In the 1840s, the settlers of Southeast Grove set aside an area of land across from the schoolhouse and designated it an official cemetery. By 1850, a Cemetery Society had been formed to manage the plots. Now, many of the early pioneers of Southeast Grove would have one of the prettiest areas of the county in which to be laid to rest. Named Southeast Grove Cemetery, this serene hilltop field would become the final resting place for many Civil War veterans and, many years later, would be rightfully called Gypsy's Graveyard. Some of those interred include William B. Post, 5th Indiana Cavalry; William H. Ketchum, 9th Indiana Infantry; Horace Durland, 5th Indiana Cavalry; David Shaffer, no citation; Henry Berdell, no citation; and James Fowler, 157th Indiana Infantry. Can this span of land be the exact same place where the gypsies buried their loved ones when they so hastily left Southeast Grove? Was this region so cursed that the small community felt the need to quarantine this plot, and only the dead were safe to inhabit it? Could there be truth to this legend?

Finding oneself traveling along on a shady country road in Lake County would bring about a sense of enjoyment—that is, unless one happens to be on South Grove Road, riding past the Southeast Grove Cemetery, the moniker for Gypsy's Graveyard atop Gypsy Hill. Weather plays no part in the atmosphere surrounding this pastoral setting. Bright sunlight cannot suppress the oppressive feeling that comes out of nowhere. The cemetery may be just a brief flash of foliage outside the window, but it has been said that the energy contained in Gypsy's Graveyard chases cars with balls of light as they wind away down the lonely road. This ball of energy, often referred to as an orb, is an anomalous globe-shaped spot, either white or colored, that appears in photographs taken at allegedly haunted locations. Orbs are commonly seen in photographs but can also be seen with the naked eye. Gypsy's Graveyard has its share of orbs within the cemetery itself and past the last row of gravestones, into the heavily wooded grounds where the bygone gypsies are rumored to be buried. Orbs that shimmer, float or move rapidly are observed regularly at Gypsy's Graveyard. Stories are told in which these anomalies are witnessed in a ray of colors, such as green, red, orange or blue. Kylee, a senior at Crown Point High School, had her experience at Gypsy's Graveyard last year: "I went there with my dad (who told me about Gypsy's), and I felt a weird atmosphere. We went back into the forest, and I heard crunching, like someone was running through the forest. But no one was there. Then I saw these red dots back there, and they were moving very quickly."

Besides eyewitness accounts of orb activity, there are a number of photographs, both developed from cameras and observed on cellphones, that suggest this cemetery is severely haunted. Bluish mists that have been observed lingering around the trees and among the headstones have been captured on camera. Occasionally, these smoke-like apparitions form a human shape and seem to glide effortlessly from grave to grave. Mists or vapors, when observed on film, can be great evidence of spirit manifestation, known as "ectoplasm." The word ectoplasm is derived from the Greek *ektos*, meaning "outside," and *plasma*, meaning "something formed or molded." This is a term coined by Charles Richet in 1894 to denote a substance of spiritual energy. It is no wonder that a spiritual energy is experienced here, given the tragic circumstances that surround this burial ground.

Cold spots, where there is a dramatic drop in temperature, are felt by the curious thrill-seeker, as well as the innocent bystander, in specific areas throughout the grave sites, no matter what the season. It is believed by ghost hunters that a ghost enables itself to manifest or make itself visible by drawing upon sources of energy, such as heat in the air. Electronic devices, including tape recorders, cameras and video equipment, using fully charged batteries have mysteriously been drained of power in and around Gypsy's Graveyard. One of the most bizarre cases was when a car battery completely died down the street as a group of young ghost hunters was exiting the area. The group stopped in front of the cemetery and began gathering their equipment for investigation. The driver got a phone call to meet the rest of his party at a nearby gas station. The plan was to return together, since one of the drivers was lost. When the ghost hunters arrived at the meeting place, their car completely lost all power, and it had to be jumped to start once more. Could it be that a spirit was preventing their return?

Sometimes spirits can become aggressive when attempting to gain the attention of the living. This has been the case at Gypsy's Graveyard, where it would seem the unsettled spirits of the gypsies feel the need to be recognized. One such occurrence happened to a young girl about twelve years ago. That experience for McKenna has caused her to "avoid the paranormal at all cost." She remembers, "I just remember going with the family [to Gypsy's Graveyard], and as we were walking around, apples were falling off the trees. Then, one flew toward me, and when we were leaving, something tugged on my dog stuffed animal."

Whispering voices seem to come from nowhere, fervently trying to communicate with whomever might be listening. Late-night visitors claim to hear unearthly voices softly calling their names. Phantom footsteps shuffle through the brush and fallen branches beyond the oldest gravestones where the native gypsies were buried. A number of EVPs (electronic voice phenomena) have been collected from Gypsy's Graveyard by novice ghost hunters, as well as more experienced paranormal investigators.

One of the most noted and mysterious phenomena that takes place in this cemetery is the claim that two of the statues on the grounds—a beautiful winged angel and a woman in a long gown—randomly disappear and reappear. The angel, prominently standing about three feet tall, has been observed on the east side of the cemetery entrance and is no longer seen there a few minutes later. The statue of a woman resembling a young gypsy girl carrying flowers is said to move about the cemetery and is seldom found in the same spot.

Since the establishment of Southeast Grove Cemetery in the early 1840s, there have been approximately 242 souls laid to rest in its tranquil location, according to a study by Ed and Doris Bruzak of Northwest Indiana's Genealogical Society in 1992. These souls have been honored and memorialized with both simple and elaborate gravestones, unlike the lot of gypsies who were abandoned in unmarked graves. A small number of modest tombstones from the early 1800s is still preserved and can be found toward the back of the cemetery. Like guardians of the restless spirits, these stones have withstood the tests of fate and time. Unfortunately, many of the markers from this same period are forever absent because of rampant vandalism at Southeast Grove Cemetery. Monuments and markers have been discovered toppled over, broken, severely damaged or missing completely. For years, this remote graveyard has been the attraction of people intent on ruination. Unfortunately, that was the case concerning a grand monument that was mentioned by Timothy H. Ball, Crown Point's noted teacher, minister and historian, in 1863: "Southeast Grove Cemetery…it contains one of the finest gray marble monuments in the county erected to the memory of Otto F. Benjamin, a very promising young man who died suddenly at the school house where he was teaching in 1871."

Ronnie Breneman, who was the chief caretaker of Southeast Grove Cemetery in 2001, was quoted in an article in the *Northwest Indiana Times* as saying that devil worshipers were drawn to Gypsy's Graveyard. He went on to recount that an occult group dug up the bones of a baby girl buried in the cemetery, stringing them from a tree with a mutilated goat and cat. It was their offering to the devil.

Gypsy's Graveyard still remains a popular place for those interested in the supernatural. Ghost hunting groups often include this legendary cemetery on their tours. The average inquisitor continues to trespass, armed with flashlights and cameras, on any given night of the week, seeking his own

Southeast Grove Cemetery warns uninvited visitors of consequences for trespassing. *Author's collection.*

ghostly experience. Nevertheless, it would seem that time has been kind to Southeast Grove Cemetery. It has returned to being a somewhat quiet resting place, with no recent incidents of foul play reported. Rob, a current officer in the patrol division for the Lake County Sheriff's Department, says none of their officers have been dispatched to that area for the last fifteen years. However, one of the Lake County sheriff's deputies remembers when his fellow deputies went on calls to Gypsy's Graveyard many years ago and told him, "That place is haunted as hell!"

The eternal residents of Southeast Grove Cemetery, also known as Gypsy's Graveyard, are destined to keep the secret of the legend of the gypsies forever. However, if the night is graced by a glowing moon and mysteries are beckoning to be solved, accept the invitation and pay your respects to the gypsies of Southeast Grove.

CHAPTER 6

HAUNTED HIGH

Oh, the glory days of high school, bringing back memories that are both nostalgic and bittersweet! Times spent with friends, classes with favorite teachers, the gratification of completing four years of studies and looking forward to a future full of possibilities are a large part of a Crown Point High School graduate's scholastic experience. Add to that list a few paranormal experiences, and you have a better account of what it was like to attend Crown Point High School.

In the mid-1800s, schools in Crown Point consisted mostly of privately funded education, established in local homes and small structures, serving approximately fifty students. Unfortunately, all these early attempts at local education, although well intended, ended in financial failure. In 1880, the school board of trustees was successful in erecting a small structure, publicly funded, to serve as the first high school in Crown Point. Called the North Ward Building, it was built on Sherman Street and served the community well until it became inadequate to accommodate the growing number of students.

Crown Point's second high school, the South Ward High School, was built in 1911. It was attended by more than six hundred students from grades seven through twelve until it also began to suffer from overcrowding. The community was in dire need of a larger building to educate its high school students.

At a special meeting of the city council in 1938, called in session by Mayor W. Vincent Youkey and attended by members of the city school board and other school officials, the mayor and councilmen gave their unanimous approval to build a new high school on an eighteen-acre plot of land on West Joliet Street. It was to be a project built with the Works Progress Administration (WPA), a government work program that was created in 1935 under U.S. president Franklin D. Roosevelt's New Deal. This program provided needed work for the millions of victims of the Great Depression, utilizing their skills and stimulating the economy. During its eight-year existence, the program employed 8.5 million people, at a cost to the federal government of approximately $11 billion. Little did the workers know that by making this location their construction site, they would be embarking on a project with dreadful circumstances.

The warm November sun made its welcome appearance on an unseasonably beautiful day in Crown Point. Although winter weather was just around the corner, there was no indication of that, as the WPA workers were scheduled to begin excavation at 104 West Joliet, the location of the new high school. That morning, the construction crew's equipment delved into the fertile soil. It was not long before one of the laborers made an unexpected discovery. Clearly noticeable were oblong shapes in the ground that had left an impression, narrow at the head and foot ends, comparable to the type of coffin used at that time. Along with clumps of soil, he unearthed several bones, arrowheads, spearheads and pottery. These remains and artifacts were promptly turned over to the health commissioner, William D. Weis, and the state archaeologist for examination. The artifacts were determined to be from the Potawatomi Indians who once inhabited the area, and the skeletal remains were human. Several of the Indian artifacts were taken to the Indiana State Museum in Indianapolis and remain on display there. A small section of Maplewood Cemetery, known as the "Paupers' Area," is now respectfully the home of the unidentified souls who were found on that autumn day.

As it turned out, Dr. Weis, as well as the school officials, was well aware of the unfortunate situation. The plot of land that the city council had purchased from John E. Luther was the prior location of a pioneer cemetery, known as Luther's Grove Cemetery. In 1853, the John and Celista Luther family deeded 1.25 acres of that land to the trustees of the Crown Point Cemetery Association for the purpose of creating a permanent cemetery. However, in 1911, the plan for this plot of land changed directions, and it was decided that the remains of the peacefully resting Crown Point occupants were to be relocated to another site that eventually became known as Maplewood Cemetery. Obvious at this point was the fact that all of the approximate two hundred bodies buried in the 1880s were not relocated. The Lake County Health Department has no records of where these remains may have gone.

"We're trying to track down where the remains went," Thomas Hawes, the part-time proprietor of Maplewood Cemetery, said. "Reports said they were moved to Maplewood Cemetery, but you can never find anything anywhere where they would have moved them."

Established in 1928, and currently located at 347 Maple Lane, Maplewood Cemetery is the final resting place for many of Crown Point's heroes and founding fathers. Colonel John Wheeler, who died at the Battle of Gettysburg, as well as United States congressman John Barney Peterson and over eighty Civil War veterans, are interred there.

Despite its dreadful beginning, Crown Point High School was dedicated to the Town of Crown Point in 1939. The exemplary light brick building consisted of classrooms on one level and presented numerous windows to welcome hundreds of anxiously awaiting students. Halls were lined with brand-new lockers against brown tile walls, and the mood was one of excitement as the doors opened for the first time in September of that same year.

Crown Point High School began reinventing itself in the early 1950s, once again breaking ground on the West Joliet site in anticipation of a much-needed gymnasium and band room. Plans also included a second story for additional classrooms and more space for future students.

In 1973, a library, auditorium, cafeteria and auxiliary gymnasium were added to the structure to accommodate Crown Point's increasing student population. Ironically, in 1975, when the construction began for a new swimming pool, another historical find astounded the city. A large trench was discovered on school property on what used to be the land owned by the Henry Wise Brickyard, the supplier of the bricks that were used in the construction of the historical Crown Point Courthouse in 1878. Glass bottles and other discarded items from the late 1800s littered the bottom of what was most likely a trash site. In addition, bandages and other medical items were found among the cluster of objects. Raising some concern was the likelihood that these items were refuse from a local apothecary during the influenza pandemic of 1890.

Disturbing grave sites and unearthing the dead can spark paranormal activity. Discovering the lingering bodies at what was once Luther's Grove Cemetery during the first stage of building Crown Point High School caused the eternal rest of the occupants to be interrupted. Add to that the fact that this land was also an "Indian burial ground," and you have the stuff

Crown Point High School, 1960s.

that legends are made of. The origins of the Indian burial ground legend came from sightings of Native American ghosts near areas that were the final resting places of local Indian tribes.

It was not until the early 1970s that paranormal activity was reported at Crown Point High School. The last phase of construction, primarily adding the auditorium, was when stories of the hauntings began. Like all auditoriums, the high school has a theatrical rigging system that enables a stage crew to safely, quickly and quietly hoist curtains, lights and scenery. Located high above the stage area are catwalks, elevated platforms that enable the theater equipment to be manipulated. During quiet times when no theater activity was scheduled, and students were far below the theater system, the hauntings of the high school began to evolve. Shadow people were witnessed lingering or silently moving from one area to the next on the catwalks. Occasionally, the ropes and pulleys, high above, would sway, as if guided by an invisible stagehand. Noises, imitating footsteps, floated down to the auditorium floor. Students felt a definite presence near the spiral staircase that wound itself high above the stage and were reluctant to tread upon it. In 1976, an impression similar to a watermark began to emerge on the ceiling of the auditorium.

Those who gazed upon the unusual phenomenon described it as the torso of a Native American. It remained there until the demolition of the high school. Could a native warrior have been standing guard over what was once his territory?

During the production of *Annie Get Your Gun*, performed by the Playmakers Community Theatre at Crown Point High School, one of the actresses experienced a ghostly visit. According to Marion Kellum, an English, drama and art teacher who taught at Crown Point High School from 1959 to 1995 and was inducted into the teacher's hall of fame in 2010, a member of the group had a paranormal experience while he was present:

> *We had finished for the day, and the auditorium was dark except for the "ghost light" being on. A ghost light illuminates the stage area for anyone unaware of the stage's drop off or orchestra pit. As I was walking with this young lady, she told me she was a sensitive, someone who is sensitive to spirits. She asked me if there were ghosts in this place. She went on to say that she felt a ghost's presence, and he was an Indian.*

Hauntings at Crown Point High School are not limited to the auditorium. By the late 1990s, students as well as teaching staff experienced paranormal activity in the gymnasium. Before and after classes, in the morning as well as early afternoon, several reports of unusual noises coming from the gymnasium were shared. Audio phenomena, described as bouncing basketballs and running footsteps along the gym floor, seemed ordinary to those students who had scheduled after-school activities, until they noticed that the gym was dark and unoccupied. Lights in the locker room and gym area would mysteriously turn on and off, with no one present to operate the switches. Nikki, who was a student in 2000 at Crown Point High School, describes her experience as "creepy": "I was a gymnast and spent a lot of evenings in the gym area, and I can definitely say that it was super creepy at night. I would hear basketballs bouncing, and locker room lights would turn on. I would never go through it [the gym] alone at night."

It is likely that this type of ghostly activity is an example of a residual haunting. These hauntings are recordings or imprints of emotionally charged past events. The spirits involved in a residual haunting are unaware of their earthly surroundings. They can be "trapped in time" and are just playing back happenings that occurred when they were alive. These events are usually deeply emotional, whether happy or sad. Everything is made up of energy, and energy cannot be destroyed. Therefore, the sights and sounds that the students and staff were witnessing in the gym at Crown Point High School could be energy that is stored in that particular area and caused by a specific event.

One such potential event took place in December 1975 at Hobart High School in Hobart, Indiana. David Gergely, a six-foot, seven-inch center for Crown Point High School, was on the basketball court competing against Hobart High. He had just completed a three-point play with six minutes to go in the game when he staggered toward the bench and collapsed. Tragically, he died shortly after. Dr. William Mott, Lake County coroner, said that David died of a congenital defect of the large vessels of the heart that would never have been detected in a routine examination.

Former classmates of David's fondly recall him as a great guy, devoted to the game of basketball. He would practice alongside his team members, day after day, perfecting his shooting skills in the Crown Point High School gymnasium. Could it be David's energy and love of the game as he was going through his repeated routine, dribbling basketballs and running up and down the court, that witnesses experienced at the high school?

Whether the haunting of Crown Point High School was reality or folklore, George Tachtiris, teacher and media center AV director, along with his AV students, produced a thirty-minute Halloween video in 1997 acknowledging the local ghost stories surrounding the high school. It was broadcast to local cable subscribers, and as Tachtiris said, "We had a little fun with the ghost stories about the high school."

Avid ghost hunters and those interested in the paranormal will, unfortunately, have no success in investigating the hallowed halls of Crown Point High School. In 1993, a new high school was proposed, and the school that was endeared by thousands of alumni was demolished in 2004. The exciting sounds of students bustling from classroom to classroom, the giddy laughter of schoolgirls, the cheers that filled the gymnasium and the banter from the teachers' lounge were forever silenced.

Colonel John Wheeler Middle School, named after a Civil War Union army hero, replaced Crown Point High School and was dedicated on Sunday, August 12, 2007. Approximately eight hundred students in grades six through eight attended the first classes there on August 23, 2007.

Do the ghosts of the old Crown Point High School still linger on the site that was once their worldly home? Have they moved on and found their eternal resting place? As time passes, the students and staff of Wheeler Middle School will be the witnesses to whether these souls have departed. At this point in time, a sense of tranquility and contentment surrounds the new structure. Perhaps sixty-five graduating classes and countless fond memories have finally healed the broken souls of the restless departed who were bound to linger within the walls of Crown Point High School.

"United We Stand, Divided We Fall," the school's motto, was adopted as the heart of Crown Point High School. Perhaps the spirits that attended the high school for decades have united and also moved on.

CHAPTER 7

LOVELY LUCREZIA

Whether one travels down South Street, Court Street, Clark Street or Main Street in Crown Point, beautiful historical homes seem to announce themselves. Prominent and breathtaking, they are beloved and admired by the people who treasure their town's history.

The Queen Anne–style mansion that is steps away from the historical Crown Point Square at 302 South Main Street is no exception. Appearing as a homestead, closer inspection reveals this handsome house as one of Crown Point's finest restaurants, Lucrezia. Introducing their guests to deliciously prepared northern Italian specialties served in an eclectic atmosphere, Michael and Nada Karas opened their dining establishment in 2003. Unbeknownst to them, when they opened their doors, they were also introducing a few ghosts.

This handsome home, whose exterior is listed in the Indiana State Register of Historical Sites and Structures, presents a façade of sage, gold and terra cotta with plum accents and features a canopied walkway. Stained-glass windows replace the sun on a cloudless day and create a mosaic rainbow on interior wooden parquet floors.

This elegant mansion was built by Italian craftsmen in 1897 and owned by a prominent citizen of Crown Point, William Barringer Brown. Much detail was given to the ornate woodwork, leaded-glass windows and sweeping staircase. The second son of Alexander Ferguson Brown and Eliza A. Barringer, William was born on June 17, 1843, in a log cabin in Southeast Grove, on land granted to his father for his

Lucrezia Café, Ristorante and Trattoria, Crown Point. *Author's collection.*

services to his country in the War of 1812. His father's death in 1849 forced William to stay with his widowed mother of five children and tend to their farm. Although it was a burdensome task at the time, it aided William in becoming a successful, wealthy and universally known dealer in hay, grain and livestock. In 1877, he was married to Carrie Sigler of Hebron, Indiana, and their union produced five children: Mary Eva, Mabel, Bernice, Bessie and Walter. In addition to managing his farming business, Brown was also director of the First National Bank of Crown Point until he died in his beloved home following a long illness in December 1924.

Mary Eva Brown, better known as "Eva," attended Western Women's College in Oxford, Ohio. She married Otto Fifield, the son of a prominent family in Crown Point, on September 22, 1910. The ceremony took place in the Browns' home and was an extravagant affair. The bridal party was introduced descending the stairway and passed through beautifully decorated rooms, and the couple was joined in matrimony by Bishop White of Michigan City, Indiana.

The Fifields enjoyed their family home at River Valley Farms, Range Line Road, south of Crown Point, until Eva inherited the Brown home in 1926. They moved their family into the elegant residence at 302 South Main Street, and shortly thereafter, it became known as Fifield Mansion. The Fifields were considered one of the most notable families in town, as Otto began his successful career in politics. In 1919–20, he was Speaker of the House of Representatives and took office as the secretary of state from 1928 to 1930. Otto Fifield ran for Congress in 1944 but was defeated by Ray Madden. He was also a delegate to the Republican National Convention in 1956 and 1960.

After accomplishing notoriety in politics, Fifield founded and was president of Otto G. Fifield, Inc., a real estate firm that was responsible for developing such subdivisions as Forest Hills, Independence Hill and Aetna in Gary, Schererville and Merrillville, Indiana.

Fifield Mansion held its distinguished name on Main Street until 1949, when it was purchased by Reed Merriam and converted to serve the community as Merriam Funeral Home. During the 1940s and 1950s, the operators of local funeral homes served as undertakers, morticians and funeral directors. They were on call twenty-four hours a day, seven days a week. They were responsible for embalming and preparing the deceased for visitation. Generally, embalming took place in the basement of the facility and visitation areas were on the main floor, with separate rooms to accommodate more than one funeral at a time. The family of the funeral director usually lived above the main visitation area.

In 1961, Reed Merriam welcomed Bernard Little as his funeral director, and for ten years, they operated the facility under the name of Merriam-Little Funeral Home. By 1974, Bernard Little and his wife, Betty, had vacated the home and decided to branch off on their own. They built a new funeral home on East Franciscan Drive, changing the name to Little Funeral Home.

The attractive mansion did not stay vacant for long. Louis Retailleau, a native-born Frenchman, and his wife, Christel, took one look at the alluring home on Main and Walnut and knew it was meant for them. In 1974, they introduced Crown Point to their new restaurant, Bon Appetit. Adorned with lace tablecloths and sparkling silver table settings, framed artwork and antique chandeliers, the formal dining room offered diners an elegant and formal atmosphere. A second room, in the rear of the house, was converted to a bistro; the tables were covered in white tablecloths, topped with butcher paper, paper lanterns and French posters, offering a separate menu. Outside, a lush garden area was available for guests to dine in a more private setting. Bon Appetit delighted diners with classic and familiar choices such as French onion soup, vichyssoise and lobster bisque. Other specialties included roasted pork loin, veal medallions and whole roasted duck in a Grand Marnier glaze. Dinner would not have been complete without Louis's famous white chocolate mousse or vanilla tarts.

The Retailleaus anticipated a glorious opening of their fine establishment, but that would not be the case. The chairs they ordered from Czechoslovakia did not arrive in time for the grand opening, and they hurriedly had to supply rental chairs to proceed with the opening. Sometime during the evening rush, while diners were enjoying their dinner, all the power in the building went out, plunging them into complete darkness. Perhaps the spirits wanted to keep the house to themselves just a little longer!

It was no secret to wait staff and other employees that the basement had been the embalming area and storage room for Merriam Funeral Home. Christel Retailleau made a few discoveries about the house on her own. Thrilled with the ornate woodwork, sweeping staircase and high ceilings, she anticipated the home to be simply perfect for her many antiques. It was not until the family moved in that she thoroughly explored the third floor. Christel shared her experience with Bill Dolan of the *Post Tribune*: "We still find hiding places and secret doors on the third floor. Our two children think it is really neat."

Despite the restaurant's shaky beginning, Bon Appetit drew patrons from miles around to relish Chef Retailleau's delicious dishes and receive his gracious hospitality for nearly thirty years. The Retailleaus occupied the residence at 302 South Main Street with their two daughters, Natalie and Sascha, until they divorced and Louis left the Midwest for San Francisco.

Michael and Nada Karas were the second restaurateurs to hold an attraction to the Fifield Mansion. They had a profitable restaurant called Lucrezia in Chesterton, Indiana, that had been open since 1997. The Karases found the history of famous femme fatale Lucrezia Borgia so intriguing that they named their restaurant in her honor. Lucrezia Borgia, born in Italy on April 18, 1480, was the illegitimate daughter of Vanozza and Pope Alexander VI. By the age of sixteen, her alleged escapades were notorious in Roman society. She was married three times; her second husband was murdered upon orders from her brother, Cesare. Her third marriage was in 1501 to Alfonso, son of the Duke of Este. Becoming the first lady of Ferrara gave Lucrezia enormous wealth and power. She became a prominent patron of the arts, attracting the flattery of poets and scholars all over Italy. Rumors

Lucrezia Borgia with her father, Pope Alexander VI, and brother, Cesare.

abounded about Lucrezia Borgia, described as a beautiful, hazel-eyed, golden-haired blonde who has been called the most depraved woman in history. She will forever be depicted as a cruel murderess who possessed a hollow ring filled with poison and used to eliminate her family's enemies. Nevertheless, she is also labeled as one of the most misunderstood femme fatales ever to have existed.

The Karases poured their time and effort into restoring what was once one of the finest mansions in Crown Point. They invested over $200,000 to ensure its success as their flagship restaurant. Preserving as many architectural details as possible, and serving rustic Italian cuisine, they accomplished their goal as a fine dining destination in November 2003.

Not long after Lucrezia opened, restaurant employees and guests began having disturbing visual experiences. Diners entering the establishment took note of a young woman, dressed in her Sunday best, descending the front staircase, only to have her disappear when she reached the bottom.

Furthermore, a man attired in a black suit and top hat has appeared frequently near the back stairs. Male patrons, glancing in the restroom mirror, have seen a gentleman behind them, although they were alone. Could these apparitions be the once honored guests of the Browns or Fifields, paying them one more visit?

Another ghostly resident of the elegantly appointed restaurant is the Lady in Red. Wait staff, going in and out of the kitchen, have witnessed the figure of a beautiful woman dressed in a long, red gown on more than one occasion. They go so far as to describe her standing with her arms crossed and tapping her foot, as if she were overseeing the restaurant's operations. By witnessing this type of apparition, the observer is most likely experiencing a residual haunting, merely a recording of past energy.

Sometimes, the energy that remains after one has passed is exhibited audibly. Noises, such as doors slamming, footsteps and even voices, can be heard in areas that absorb natural energy. A server at Lucrezia recalls a night, several years ago, that was very memorable to him:

> *I was closing the restaurant one night. Everyone had left, and I was finishing up the day by going to the office. It's in the basement. There's a vent down there, an air vent, and as I was finishing up, I heard footsteps above me. They sounded like someone was walking with heavy boots. The first thing I thought of was maybe the kitchen help had come back for something. So, I go up the stairs and I said, "Hey, I locked up for the night, no one is supposed to be here." I went to the kitchen, and no one. I was alone. I had always heard stories from other people who work here and stories in general about this place being haunted. I wanted to experience something for myself. Now, for sure, I knew that I had, and wow, it was scary. I never had anything happen to me after that, but that was enough.*

One summer evening, a guest was being seated by the restaurant's hostess at an elegantly set table that was in the center room, across from the bar. The menus were delivered, and soon the dinner guest motioned for the waitress to come over to the table. She told the waitress that she was a sensitive, and despite the warm and inviting atmosphere, she was feeling uncomfortable. She went on to tell the waitress that she was being bombarded by whispering voices that wanted to communicate with her. At the guest's request, the hostess reseated her on the outside patio, where she could enjoy her dinner in peace and quiet!

Highly sensitive people have an increased susceptibility to stimulation. They process odors, sounds and even feelings more deeply than others. In the paranormal world, they are said to possess a sixth sense, which is the ability to perceive the subtle dimension, or the unseen world of ghosts, angels and so on. Most people perceive the seen world through their five physical senses: sight, hearing, touch, smell and taste. By possessing a sixth sense, one has an extrasensory perception of information not gained through the recognized senses. Who were all the spirits trying to communicate with the sensitive diner? Were they the souls of the dearly departed who once rested at the Merriam Funeral Home?

Regardless of the candescent parquet floor, mosaic tiled bar and cozy Italian atmosphere of Lucrezia, many guests who feast on their traditional signature dishes undergo more than just an enchanting night out. Ascending the wooden steps and entering the reception area often produces two reactions to one's surroundings. First, the appreciation of the beautifully preserved staircase, commonly followed by an emotional or physical response. Several locations on the main floor of the old mansion emanate significant drops in temperature or cause flu-like symptoms, such as nausea and dizziness. This is considered by some to be due to a rise and drop of energy in the surrounding environment and can indicate the possibility of attempted ghostly communication. One can also feel the residual energy of souls who have passed by experiencing a strong emotion, such as sadness, fear or even extreme joy.

One such occurrence happened to a dinner guest seated in a small alcove in the rear of the restaurant. She encountered a severe drop in temperature and became so disoriented that she could not focus on the menu in front of her. After a few moments and a few deep breaths, her symptoms subsided, and she continued her evening. Was this guest merely sensing the deceased that once rested at the Merriam Funeral Home?

Occasionally, spirits interact with the living in intelligent hauntings, which involve ghostly spirits communicating or interfering with the living on the earthly plane. These entities are believed to remain behind for several reasons, including unfinished business, re-living traumatic events, fear of crossing over to the other side or simply not being aware that their physical body has expired. A patron remembers an actual interaction with a ghost while he dined at Lucrezia:

> *Once, when we went there, we ordered from a waiter named James. We then waited for quite some time, and our order didn't arrive. I called another*

waiter named John and asked what was holding up our order. He told us he was sorry and asked us what the name of our waiter was. We said James. He replied, "That can't be, because James passed away a year ago."

A warm summer evening turned out to be a cooling experience for one particular teenager who was standing on the front steps outside the restaurant. Having expressed her reluctance to enter the building because of its history, she suddenly witnessed her necklace and bracelet coming detached and falling to the ground at the same time.

Evidence of Lucrezia's hauntings was collected by a local paranormal group that investigated the building. The ghost hunters recovered several EVPs of disembodied voices. Researchers believe that voices of the deceased can be recorded on audiotape and played back. Sometimes amplification and filtering can produce sounds not heard at the time of the recording. Many paranormal investigators use this method to communicate with spirits, asking questions to receive an audio response.

For almost a century, the house at 302 South Main Street has hosted significant events in the lives of many of the families of Crown Point. It has rendered pride, joy, success and sadness for the living, as well as for the souls who will forever remain behind.

Whether one's visit to Lucrezia provides a ghostly encounter or simply an entertaining evening out, no one has ever left disappointed. In fact, some guests have never left at all.

CHAPTER 8

THE HOUSE ON RUFFLE SHIRT HILL

Being among the oldest towns in Lake County, it is no wonder that Crown Point charms both the visitor and the resident with its delightful balance of old and new. This mixture is evident in the Crown Point Square, as well as the surrounding neighborhoods. One only has to travel north on Main Street to marvel at the historical buildings on the Square and then spy the modern, high-air supported sports structure, called the Dome.

Crown Point citizens appreciate their architectural heritage and have gone to great lengths to care for and preserve countless commercial buildings and homes throughout the region. The Crown Point Courthouse Square District has at least thirty-eight out of fifty buildings in the boundary listed as being historically significant.

If stately homes from eras gone by enthrall the typical visitor, he will be enchanted by the numerous residences listed in the National Register of Historic Places. To attain this honor, the building must be nominated and submitted to the Historic Preservation and Archaeological Division of the Department of Natural Resources and sent to the State Review Board. The building must be restored as much as possible to its original look, including interior and exterior. If the structure passes the required tests, the application is sent to Washington, D.C., for signature by U.S. Department of the Interior officials.

In 1998, the Greater Crown Point Chamber of Commerce conducted a two-mile, self-guided walking tour of some of the city's historical homes. Walkers, equipped with the colorful brochure that featured photographs, as well as descriptions of about thirty homes along Court and South Streets, were enthralled by the various styles from the past.

Strolling or driving leisurely along shady, tree-lined South Court Street, just south of the Crown Point Square, creates a feeling of nostalgic peacefulness. Its stately homes from the late eighteenth and early nineteenth centuries are among those listed in the National Register of Historic Places and are a true example of the growing economy of Crown Point during that time.

The coming of the railroad to Crown Point in the early 1900s provided businesses and area farmers greater access to markets such as Chicago, and their profits were gaining. Successful businessmen and merchants were attracted to neighborhoods in proximity to the Crown Point downtown area, and soon the prominent homes on South Court Street were erected. Generous-sized lots, deeply set back from the street, were perfect for creating a gracious, quiet atmosphere.

The 1920s was the decade that modernized America. The increase in popular entertainment and consumerism was the general cause for a feeling of great optimism. Flamboyancy and frivolity were profoundly prominent in fashion and behavior. Although liquor was outlawed during Prohibition, drinking and smoking heavily occurred behind closed doors.

It was around this time that South Court Street, home to the elite upper social class of Crown Point, became the topic of conversation, as it drew one particular newspaper publisher's attention. This particular publisher labeled this notorious street "Ruffle Shirt Hill," implying its residents were uppity members of society who would have worn ruffled shirts (ruffled shirts were attire worn by wealthy gentlemen during colonial times). With this expression, he also insinuated this group of neighbors was cliquish, threw lavish parties and had loose morals.

One simply has to visit South Court Street today to understand how it reflects the elaborate and extravagant lifestyle of the 1920s and imagine its storybook past. Although most of the residences were built from 1890 to 1920, several homes dating back to the mid-1800s still captivate their audience with their timeless aura. From the district's oldest homes at 355 and 481 South Court Street, built in 1860, to those erected from 1890 to 1936, an appreciation for an important period in Crown Point's history can undoubtedly be gained.

Tranquil as this nostalgic neighborhood may be, disturbing rumors and untold secrets can almost be heard echoing through the trees, and especially from one house on Ruffle Shirt Hill. Standing on the grassy edge of the

Bicycling down South Court Street, 1907. *Courtesy of Lake County, Indiana Historical Society.*

property at 446 South Court Street does not immediately send a chill down one's spine or trigger an uncomfortable response, but nonetheless, this pre–American Civil War home is haunted. Presenting a stucco over brick façade, the house contains a whimsical door and tall, narrow windows that create a warm, cottage-like atmosphere. Next, however, one's eyes are drawn upward to the cross-gabled, steeply pitched roofline and one small, dark attic window that evokes quite the opposite feeling.

Interestingly enough, the front of this house, facing South Court Street, was originally the rear, and the back garden entrance faces Main Street to the east. Typical of homes from this period, 446 South Court Street has three levels, separating public and private spaces. The main floor contains rooms that were once a formal parlor, dining area and kitchen. These rooms, in addition to front halls, were considered public areas. The parlor, where guests were received and entertained, was presented as the best room in the house, decorated lavishly to boast of the owner's wealth and position. The kitchen was offset, so as not to be seen from the parlor, keeping the servants away from the view of the guests.

Ascending the ninety-degree staircase to the second floor brings one to a loft area and four rooms. During the late eighteenth century, bedrooms were usually located on an upper floor and were called chambers. Homes had three to four chambers, where occupants would disrobe, sleep for the night and then awaken, dress and prepare for the day. Rooms labeled as bedrooms were actually "fainting rooms," containing a day bed, where occupants would merely rest for brief periods during the day.

The outbreak of the Civil War in 1861 began as a struggle to preserve the Union, not a struggle to free the slaves, but ultimately, the conflict would decide both issues. It was during the thirty years prior to the Civil War that the Underground Railroad provided freedom to slaves from Southern states, where the practice of slavery was legal. The "railroad" was a network used by enslaved black Americans and provided by abolitionists. Abolitionists were opposed to slavery and enabled the slaves to escape to the Northern states and Canada. Using the terminology of the railroad, those who guided slaves to safety and freedom were called "conductors," and the slaves were "passengers." Homes where fugitive passengers could safely hide were "stations."

Surreptitiously, in 1858, two homes on Ruffle Street Hill were "stations," and 446 South Court Street was one of them. The Underground Railroad was not a series of underground tunnels. The stations were actually places where people had secret rooms or concealed spaces to harbor "passengers" before they were guided to freedom. This home clearly has hidden areas and mysterious doors where one can picture the runaway slaves who were harbored.

The basement at 446 South Court Street is a combination of rooms that still contain the brick and dirt floors from the original house built in 1858. Maids and servants of the household resided here, as was typical of the wait staff in the late 1800s. Dense, heavy metal doors remain behind, suggesting that they guarded entry into spaces that were once the brief housing for slaves traveling along the Underground Railroad.

Amanda, the current owner of the property, has very strong emotions regarding the basement area. An uncomfortably fearful feeling has been with her since the day she and her husband explored it. To her amazement, several pieces of furniture and other items were simply left in various rooms of the basement by previous owners. One room in particular has a cold undercurrent and is cluttered with items from centuries gone by. She says, "I never go down [in] the basement myself, and I am comfortable in the house itself. The previous owner also felt the same. She wouldn't go down to the basement by herself."

At the top of the stairs, through a wooden door, a mysterious room awaits the visitor to 446 South Court Street. An attic-like space, created by the steep roofline, reveals a room with two small doors set in opposite walls. Passage through these inconspicuous doorways reveals small, windowless, dark areas. Were these spaces merely for storage, or was this upper room designed with the intention of providing hidden temporary quarters for runaway slaves? One door refuses to remain shut and is a constant concern for the current owner. Despite closing the door and making sure it is secure, she often discovers the little door to be wide open:

> *This is one of the most unsettling things when I came here, to the point that I would have tears in my eyes. I keep that door shut. The door likes to open up. One day I came up here, and it was all the way opened up. Then I would shut it, and it would kind of stick, and it's a light door....And the weird thing is that sometimes it would be slightly open, and sometimes all the way open, against the wall. So what I've done for the last year is put something in front of it, heavy books. It opens with the books on the floor!*

Could the long-gone spirits of the "passengers" be sending the message that they are ready to go?

In 1870, the Underground Railroad reached its symbolic end, as the Fifteenth Amendment to the Constitution extended suffrage to African American men. It was during this period that the house at 446 South Court Street was sold to an elite citizen of Crown Point. It was the perfect home for William Allen Scheddell and his wife, Mabel. He was an established pharmacist, with a successful business on the Square. Scheddell and Wendt Bros. Pharmacy, located at 104 South Main Street, provided pharmaceuticals and homemade remedies such as camphorated oil and rosewater, along with everyday necessities. The lady of the house could also purchase books, paints, wallpaper and fancy toiletries from this prestigious drug establishment.

Soon after acquiring their home, the Scheddells fondly named it Tarn (lake) Cottage and embellished the façade with a green oval plaque that proudly displayed its name and the year it was built. Unfortunately, William and Mabel's life together at Tarn Cottage was cut short in 1920. On the cold evening of January 13, 1920, William died while walking home from work on the Crown Point Square.

As was customary in the 1920s, William's body was displayed in the front parlor of 446 South Court Street, where friends and family of the Scheddells could call and offer their condolences. Scheddell was laid to rest in Maplewood Cemetery, where he remains today. After William's death, his wife was joined at the residence by her sister, Alice Upham. Alice, an avid horticulturalist, created a whimsical rose garden in the east yard, with over ten rose beds. Her roses won national acclaim in the 1940s, as she was featured in the Depression edition of *Better Homes and Gardens*. Before leaving the Crown Point area, Mabel discovered several of her husband, William's, private journals hidden at his pharmacy in the Crown Point Square. Soon after confiscating them, Mabel was sure to sell them. What was written by William that was so secretive that he felt compelled to conceal them? Could William have experienced some paranormal activity himself at his new home that was embarrassing to his wife?

The house at 446 South Court Street was acquainted with many owners, and it also sat abandoned for many years. Documentation indicates it has had at least nine recorded owners.

It was during one of its latest renovations, before Amanda and her family took possession of the home, that a young woman, Sally, had a harrowing experience. She was familiar with many homes on Ruffle Shirt Hill because she offered a cleaning service to the owners. When the new owners of 446 South Court Street asked her to help them prepare the home by doing some painting, she and a partner gladly accepted the job. It was on one particular evening when the ladies were performing their painting duties that Sally recalls her paranormal incident:

> *I was painting upstairs, and my friend Heidi was downstairs. I turned and saw a lady in a black, bustled dress, similar to the 1900s, floating up the stairs. I called out to my friend, "Where are you?" because I thought, could this be her? She called to me and said she was downstairs working. Then she came upstairs with me, and I told her what I saw. Right after that, we heard a clanging sound. The house has a slot that serves as a mailbox. We thought it was someone outside lifting the door on the mailbox. We went downstairs to look in the slot, and there was nothing there. Then we spotted the fireplace tools, shook them and re-created the sound. I started back up the stairs, with Heidi behind me, when we heard that clang again. Heidi ran past me so fast on the stairs, I thought she was going to knock me down!*

Since Amanda, her husband and their two children have occupied the home, about a year ago, they have experienced several unsettling occurrences. On the first night their teenage daughter settled into her bedroom, located at the back of the house on the first floor, she became aware of a strong presence. She felt something was trying to communicate that she was not welcome in this particular area. One late night, as Amanda's daughter lay in bed, she heard a rustling sound, over and over again. It seemed to come from an old vent leading directly to the basement. The family immediately performed a thorough investigation of the basement and found nothing that could be attributed to the sound. This rustling was repeated for several nights and came not only from the vent but also deep in the room's closet. Could the spirits of the runaway slaves from the Underground Railroad still be afraid of being discovered, or are they merely whispering to one another?

Upstairs, on the second-floor landing, some of the guests at 446 South Court Street have reported feeling anxious or dizzy. It is widely believed by paranormal researchers that ghosts can create an electromagnetic field that is stronger than what is produced by electrical wiring, outlets and electrical appliances.

While replacing insulation in one of the upstairs bedrooms, Amanda's husband took a picture of the exposed space between the walls, and what appeared in the photograph was the large face of a man with dark eyes and a black mustache. Amanda described:

> *It appeared to me in the picture that this was a dark man, maybe an African American man, just watching. Watching someone or something. I felt I needed to speak to him, to stop the paranormal activity in my home. I told him I was now the steward of this home, and I would bring it back to its glory. It seemed to help, and soon we all felt much better.*

Furthermore, there is an unexplainable mystery about the doors at 446 South Court Street. In addition to the doors that concealed secretive rooms throughout the home, one particular door is quite disturbing to its owners. Located in the master bedroom, halfway up the wall, is a small cabinet-like door, painted over by its previous owners. It remains hidden behind Amanda's headboard, and she has not been eager to discover the mystery that lies behind it. Puzzling to the current owners is the reason why all the doors on the closets, as well as the kitchen cabinets, have been removed.

Amanda had gotten an extremely negative feeling while in her bedroom during the first months she moved in. It was in the bedroom, when she was alone one night, that she experienced a haunting. Tucked in bed with her dog, India, lying near her on the floor, Amanda was catching up on her daily paperwork. She remembers:

It was

Dedication plaque to Ruffle Shirt Hill unveiled by Charles and Mabel Swisher on June 1, 1976.

The dog in Lamson's yard, Crown Point's most famous landmark. *Author's collection.*

around 2:30 or 3:00 a.m. that I was interrupted by the sound of a thick metal door dragging and then slamming. It was so loud, it seemed to come from the center of the house. It scared me. I imagined a door dragging on concrete. After a few minutes, it slammed a second time. I knew India heard it too; he jumped into bed with me and was shaking.

Amanda and her family have constant confirmation that their pre–Civil War home is indeed haunted. Keys that stopped working, unexplained noises, doors opening on their own and stories from previous owners about clocks that have all stopped at the same time every day only validate what they have known since the day they crossed the threshold.

Tales have also been told of a mysterious house on South Court Street rumored to have been a prison for a physically and mentally handicapped child during the late 1800s. Worried that this unfortunate child would embarrass the family, they barred her bedroom window and kept her hidden from the neighbors. It was not until the child died of neglect that the community discovered the existence of the little girl. Years later, neighbors claimed to have heard music and voices coming from the home.

Walking past 487 South Court Street on any given moonlit night has been known to produce a ghostly apparition for the curious spirit-seeker. The Luther family, who owned property on Ruffle Shirt Hill during the 1900s, memorialized their family dog by placing a replica of the pet on their front lawn. The statue is known as "the dog in Lamson's Yard" and is said to bark at passersby when the Crown Point Courthouse clock tower strikes midnight. Some residents also believe that the dog prevents children from getting hit by passing cars. Legend has it that the pet is actually trapped inside the prominent statue.

Given the history and mystery that surrounds the street fondly known as Ruffle Shirt Hill, what better place could there be for a scary ghost story?

CHAPTER 9

ZOMBIES AND "SPIRITS"

It is easy to become immersed in the Polynesian atmosphere of a quaint bar nestled in the corner of the north side of the Crown Point Square, called the Zombie Club. Adorned in island décor and soothing lighting, this bar gently eases the visitor into the South Pacific nightclub atmosphere. The Zombie Club is what is known as a tiki bar.

Tiki bars were drinking establishments during the 1950s and 1960s that popularized the theme of thatched roofs, rattan furniture, bright colors and torches that reflected the Polynesian culture. The popular tiki culture began in the United States with the opening of a Hollywood bar in 1934 called Don the Beachcomber, owned and operated by Ernest Raymond Beaumont Gantt. Ernest, who later changed his name to Donn Beach, was excited to implement his experiences from his Asian travels by creating a Tahitian-style restaurant displaying his souvenirs and serving exotic rum cocktails. This establishment soon became the hot spot for Hollywood elite, and the tiki style swept the nation in popularity. This expressive style of island flavor became more than just a decorative tool; it suggested a lifestyle. Enjoying dinner or having a drink in a tiki bar was meant to transport one mentally to a tropical paradise, where one could relax to tranquilizing melodies, sip exotic cocktails and almost feel the warm breeze of the ocean.

Pam Porter-Tufo's lifelong dream was to own a restaurant/bar in her hometown. When Pam and her husband, Ron, saw potential in the tavern called Sidekicks, located at 118 South Clark Street, they purchased the building in 2001. Sidekicks drew an older crowd to the Square, but that was

Zombie Club. *Author's collection.*

about to change. Pam wanted to create a venue in honor of her grandfather that would bear the same name as the bar he owned in the late 1940s, called the Zombie Club.

John Anello opened the Zombie Club in Harvey, Illinois, in 1948, shortly after he was released from jail for bootlegging—or distributing liquor without registration or payment of taxes—on the South Side of Chicago. The majority of taverns in that decade became more successful when attributed to the owner, so John soon changed the name of his bar to Anello's. Anello's was a favorite spot for fifty years in the Chicago Heights area and was also remembered as being called the Blue Ribbon, given the nickname from a Pabst Blue Ribbon sign he hung in front of the building.

Pam quickly began disassembling Sidekicks, completely changing the décor, apart from the tin ceilings and brick walls. The bar was painted gold to contrast the dark brick walls, giving the appearance of a tropical yet elegant paradise. She surrounded the long, dark wood bar with bamboo tables and chairs, nestled under grass-topped tiki huts. At the very back of the room, slightly out of place but offering a comfortable place to relax, a fireplace was installed. Comfortable leather couches sat across from the fire, where one could absorb the relaxing atmosphere. Pam's final touches included tropical plants and orchids placed near the back walls.

Pam's vision came to life with the introduction of the Zombie Club to the historical Crown Point Square, but ironically, so did the souls who might have remained there for years. The bartenders and wait staff will be the first to admit they are serving up more than just alcoholic "spirits" at the Zombie Club. They have had experiences that they attribute to supernatural activity present in the bar.

Alone, before operating hours, is usually a peaceful time to prepare for the lunch crowd that will descend around noon—unless the ghosts decide to make themselves the first guests. Retrieving liquor, beer and wine from the basement is one task that most employees dread. It is common for them to hear not only the front door open and slam shut but also footsteps from above. Upon returning upstairs, the bartenders find the doors, in fact, locked and no one there but themselves.

Each restroom in the rear of the bar displays a large, gold-framed mirror above the sink to assure the guests they are looking their best. Perhaps there is a narcissistic ghost, only interested in his own reflection, that has kept annoying the bar's management. For years, keeping a mirror in the men's restroom has been a challenge. Strangely enough, it either falls from the wall and shatters, displays large cracks or disappears completely.

The general atmosphere at the Zombie Club is lively and upbeat, especially when it has guest musical performances. Entering the front half or sitting at the bar does not usually bring about any sense of uneasiness, but proceeding to the back, primarily around the fireplace, is a different story. Almost immediately, one who is somewhat sensitive can feel a buzz of energy surround him. Guests have experienced tingling throughout their body, a feeling of paranoia or a dull headache that will not subside. Other physical manifestations, like dizziness and nausea, occur just outside the men's restroom.

Orbs, swiftly moving in straight lines, have been captured on security cameras in these same areas in the rear of the bar. Many believers in the paranormal feel these small specks of circular light are human spirits in the form of balls of energy. Stationary orbs, which manifest in clear, white and light blue colors, are also present in photographs taken by cameras and camera phones. A good number of these orbs have made their appearance on the ceiling outside the rear exit door. Theories on the color of orbs by members of the paranormal field can give a better understanding of what they might mean. It is speculated that clear orbs are past spirits communicating the experience of a significant event that took place in that location and their desire for guidance to move on. White orbs are believed to be trapped spirits, there to provide protection, and blue orbs are believed to be heavenly, calm spirits.

An interesting EVP was seized by a young woman on a recent ghost tour at the Zombie Club. Toward the end of the night, when the bar was almost empty, her recording revealed the high-pitched sound of female laughter. There were no female patrons in the bar at the time who could have produced this outcome. It was suggested she try once again, and after reviewing the second recording, the voice was still present.

This type of EVP is evidence of a residual haunting. Energy from an emotionally charged event imprints itself on the atmosphere. This suggests a spirit is performing or reliving an experience over and over without being aware of its environment. The audio demonstration of female laughter, acquired from the Zombie Club, is most likely the impression of a lively spirit.

During a recent ghost tour featuring the Zombie Club, a photograph was taken of guests seated next to the fireplace. It captured an enormous cloud of mist swirling just above them. Ghostly vapors or mists, commonly known as ecto-mists, can be evidence of ghostly manifestations. They can take on the appearance of a human shape but often appear as a cloud or haze. Although not seen by the naked eye, they become evident in photographs.

The most puzzling phenomenon contributing to the characteristics of this haunted location is the discovery of what could be a possible portal, where spirits can travel from the supernatural world into the physical world. The existence of a portal can rely on a vortex of energy to sustain it. This is a high concentration of powerful spiritual energy, which can be positive or negative in nature. Vortexes tend to exist where there are strong concentrations of gravitational anomalies. This, in turn, creates an area that can bend light and cause a considerable distortion in the human energy field. They have also been shown to be associated with ley lines and have been found to be considerably stronger at node points, where several ley lines cross. Mirrors can act as man-made portals to the other side. Old mirrors are constructed with a silver metal backing, which has the highest electrical and thermal conductivity of any metal and one of the greatest levels of optical reflectivity available. Light being an electromagnetic field and the fact that spirits operate at high ultraviolet frequencies increase the likelihood that these entities would be attracted to a mirror and ultimately pass through from the physical to the spiritual world.

There are two different kinds of portals, based on the nature and direction of the flow of energy. They can be positive, where energy flows upward, from out of the earth, dispersing electric energy and revitalizing the spirit. They can also be negative, where energy flows inward, toward the earth, creating feelings of fear, confusion, anger, hate, jealousy or even depression.

Mounted high on the back walls of the Zombie Club is a captivating collection of vintage mirrors. One large mirror, located above the fireplace, suggests the possible existence of such a portal. Random photographs clearly show the frame of vertical and horizontal lines within the reflection of the mirror. Can this be a doorway for entities to enter the physical world or a path for lost souls to leave the earth and find their way to the other side?

The property at 118 South Clark Street, built in 1920, has been a neighborhood tavern since the end of Prohibition. Becoming one of the first destinations for the legal sale and consumption of alcohol on the Crown Point Square, the Schlitz Tavern opened in 1935.

Five years later, one of Crown Point's upstanding residents, John Boe, purchased the building and moved into the upstairs apartment with his wife, Minnie, and son, John Jr. Hard work and a lifelong dream turned the space below into Boe's Bar. Surrounded by a tin ceiling and wooden floor, the working class gathered for good conversation, whiskey and beer. On late afternoons, seats at the bar were occupied by men in dusty work clothes, fedoras and ball caps, enjoying a drink or two before heading home.

The bar changed hands again in 1946, when it became Clem's, owned by Clem Gremel. Then, in the late 1950s, Ed Cassaday became the proprietor and left many Crown Point residents with fond memories of a friendly bar that served great food.

Ironically, Ed Cassaday had ties to the South Pacific, where he served as a paratrooper in the U.S. Marine Corps during World War II. He was awarded the Purple Heart medal and applied his never-quit attitude to his business, rightly named Ed's Place. Ed's was just the sort of tavern where neighbors could kick back and enjoy his famous cornmeal pizza. Ed's Place was in business until 1974, when a "for sale" sign was posted in the window once again.

Throughout the late 1980s, 118 South Clark Street transitioned into the Gridiron Bar and Grill, catering to the blue-collar crowd. This was a time when the nation focused on the dangerous consequences of drinking and driving. Trace Embry, owner and operator of the Guardian Escort Service,

Boe's Tavern, 1930s. *Courtesy of Lake County, Indiana Historical Society.*

feeling compelled to address his concern on this issue, made the Gridiron his "home base," where he offered his free driving services to those who felt the need for a ride home.

Changing owners once again, in 1987, the bar became Sidekicks. It remained Sidekicks until it became what it is known as today, the Zombie Club.

The Zombie Club has become one of the major bars/restaurants on the Crown Point Square, where one can enjoy great food, drinks and entertainment. Just walking in the door, passing the tiki hut on the right and sitting either at the bar or among the tropical plants at a table creates the excitement of the South Pacific. This club provides quite a different kind of excitement for the avid ghost hunter, but nonetheless, everyone finds the "spirits" at this club stimulating. Pam Porter-Tufo invites her guests to settle in and order her intriguing signature drink, made with three kinds of rum: pineapple, papaya and lime juice. Of course, it's called a "Zombie"!

CHAPTER 10

THE IMPRISONED SOULS OF THE CROWN POINT JAIL

Every building is composed of basic materials: concrete, wood, bricks and nails. They all have the sole purpose of coming together as one to create a structure. Jails and prisons are not evil, but with the passing of time, can they absorb the despair, pain and torment of the misguided prisoners who were confined there? Negative energy can leave an imprint on its surroundings, especially if strong emotions exist. People who have experienced violence, cruelty, abuse and even confusion can leave their opposing energy behind, resulting in a residual haunting, where spirits are unaware that they have died. In other instances, lost souls can feel bound to this world and have a problem crossing over because they fear what awaits them on the other side or they themselves are waiting for some retribution for what they have done. Hundreds of malevolent souls once walked the halls and occupied the cells at the historic Crown Point Jail, located at 231 Joliet Street. Although these cells remain empty and the building is no longer used as a prison, tormented voices continue to cry out, begging to be heard.

Crown Point's first jail was erected in 1851 as an addition to the first Lake County Courthouse on Clark Street. It was small and constructed with heavy hardwood cross wooden planking, containing only a few iron cells. The most common crime during this time was horse stealing, punishable by a fine of $50 to $100 and in some cases necessitating a lashing. Disorderly conduct, gambling and drunkenness were also punishable by fine, and if they were not promptly paid, the offender found himself serving his sentence in the Crown Point Jail.

As the population of the seat of Lake County grew, the need for a larger courthouse and jail became evident. In 1882, Beers and Beer, a prominent construction company located in Chicago, was hired to build the new sheriff's house and adjoining jail at 226 South Main Street. Indiana law at that time required county sheriffs to live adjacent to or within the property of their jail.

The sheriff's house adopted the Second Empire style, which originated in Paris and was becoming the most modern trend for public buildings and homes in America. The house displayed a mansard roof, which was the major defining element of the Second Empire style, with decorative eave brackets with round heads and highly embellished surrounds. The jail measured thirty-six by forty-eight feet and contained ten steel cells along steel corridors, six for male prisoners and four for females.

It was in one of these dark, musty cells in the back of the jail that Armin Bendick found himself on a hot evening in August 1900. For nearly a month he was held, existing on only bread and water, in a secret plot to dispose of him by his business rival. Bendick was rescued by passing a note in the shoe of a discharged prisoner, but not before he gnawed at the wooden boards and iron bars of his cell.

Sheriff's house and jail, built in 1882, in the Second Empire style.

Sheriff's house on a shady summer afternoon, 1960s.

In 1910, the jail was replaced by a larger facility, measuring 50 by 120 feet. Here, criminal offenders were detained, awaiting their trial or receiving punishment for petty crimes with a short term of confinement. Cellblocks, or multiple jail cells, were arranged adjacent to a common area. Prisoners could move about the common area for recreation and exercise periods. Meals for the inmates were delivered through small openings in the cell bars. Guards were in charge of accounting for the prisoners and made their rounds when the sun went down.

A tour guide who spends a vast amount of time in the Crown Point Jail believes that the jail is, indeed, haunted by a past security guard. She says she has been chased out of the jail many times and one time, while sitting on a bench from 1908, was hit by an invisible force so strong it lifted the bench from the floor.

Stories of glowing flickers of light, slowly moving past the windows in the jail, have been reported by several people passing through the courtyard between the Halls of Justice and the jail. One Crown Point resident who frequently enjoys dinner and drinks on the Square recounts her disturbing experience as she passed by the jail one evening in the summer of 2016:

I was walking past the jail with my friend, on our way to have dinner at Lucrezia, when we noticed a flicker of like an amber light coming from the windows of the jail. It was moving from the front of the jail to the back at kind of a steady pace. We said it reminded us of a night watchman, from back in the day, holding his lantern and making his way past the rows of prisoners.

On January 29, 1919, Congress ratified the Eighteenth Amendment to the Constitution, which prohibited the manufacturing, transportation and sale of alcohol within the United States. This period, known as Prohibition, lasted from 1920 to 1933 and opened the door for the gangster era. Average citizens found themselves turning to illegal activity. Organized crime thrived, and the American mobster was looked upon by common people as a hero. Local crime was on the rise, as residents began making moonshine or bathtub gin in their homes. Speakeasies, illegal drinking spots, were disguised with storefronts around the Crown Point Square.

In 1928, a second addition was made to the rear of the sheriff's house, through the block to East Street. The building now supported a larger area for the sheriff and his family, the warden's residence and department offices. With the completion of the addition, the total capacity of the building accommodated approximately one hundred prisoners. Two different-sized prison cells were designed; some of the cells were for four inmates, and some were for two inmates. In this addition of the jail, cellblocks were arranged adjacent to a day room, providing recreation and meals. The new Crown Point Jail was considered the finest incarceration facility in Indiana and was thought to be escape-proof.

The following year, in 1929, the State of Indiana built the Halls of Justice, adjacent to the sheriff's house and jail. As Lake County's Criminal Courts building, this twenty-thousand-square-foot structure was connected to the jail by way of an underground tunnel. Criminal cases were brought here before the judge for arraignment and trial. Following their appointment in court, the defendants were transported back to the jail discreetly by way of the tunnel or elevated bridge. The bridge that supplied another pathway between the Halls of Justice and the jail began just outside the door from the holding cells on the second floor of the courtroom. It was built as another safe option of transportation between the buildings.

The city of Crown Point is well known for the incarceration of infamous gangster John Dillinger and his escape from the Crown Point Jail in 1939.

However, fifteen years earlier, another infamous gangster was in the local headlines.

Frank McErlane began his nefarious career in 1913, when he was sent to prison for his involvement in a car theft ring. By 1922, he was once again a free man and had become affiliated with such famous gangsters as Joseph "Polack Joe" Saltis, Johnny "The Fox" Torrio and Al Capone, running on the South Side of Chicago. He was known as an alcoholic and a compulsive killer. Frank McErlane and two of his friends, John O'Reilly and Alex McCabe, happened to be at a halfway house between Cedar Lake and Crown Point on May 4, 1924, when he accepted a challenge to prove his marksmanship skills. Unfortunately, local attorney Thaddeus S. Fancher was also there, having a drink that proved to be his last. He became Frank's chosen target and was shot down in cold blood with a single bullet to the head. McErlane escaped indictment, while O'Reilly eventually was convicted of the murder and was sentenced to life in prison. McCabe received a life sentence as well but was later acquitted because an eyewitness to the crime, Frank Cochran, was unable to testify. Cochran's body was found on the property of the Crown Brewing Company on Goldsborough Street in Crown Point, with his head split in two by an axe. In August 1926, Frank McErlane was finally taken into custody by the Lake County sheriff, but his trial was moved to Porter County, Indiana. He was never convicted of the murder of Thad Fancher.

The failure of the federal government and local law enforcement to enforce Prohibition led to the adoption in 1933 of the Twenty-First Amendment to the Constitution, which repealed the Eighteenth Amendment. The creation of Prohibition surprisingly increased alcohol consumption, led to organized crime by bootlegging and resulted in the federal and state governments losing billions of dollars in tax revenue.

With liquor legalized once again, gangs were forced to seek other options for making money illegally. Gambling, narcotics trafficking and bank robbery became more lucrative. One of the gangs making its presence known in Chicago and northwest Indiana was the Pierpont Gang. Composed of Harry Pierpont, Homer Van Meter and John Dillinger, it was considered one of the most deadly bank robbery gangs in the country. These gangsters quickly gained notoriety not only for their exploits but also for the way they dressed. Wearing dark overcoats and wide-brimmed hats pulled down low to hide their identities, they were confident and precise when it came to bank robbery. The Pierpont Gang, also known as the Dillinger Gang, acquired over $160,000 in stolen cash before they planned the bank robbery in East Chicago that would ultimately lead John Dillinger to the jail in Crown Point.

Violence was not John Dillinger's style, but on January 15, 1934, at 2:50 p.m., he committed his first and only murder. While robbing the First National Bank in East Chicago, Indiana, Dillinger was fired upon by East Chicago patrolman William Patrick O'Malley as he was walking with fellow gang members to the getaway car. Dillinger's bulletproof vest proved to be a lifesaver, as he turned and shot O'Malley eight times across the chest, causing his death. Dillinger continued his gunfire until the getaway car pulled away, its door torn off by a car parked along the street. John Dillinger was officially charged with O'Malley's murder. The gang escaped first to Florida, then to El Paso, Texas, and finally to the Hotel Congress in Tucson, Arizona.

John Dillinger was arrested on January 21, 1934, by Tucson police, while in possession of $7,175.44, which included money stolen from the First National Bank in East Chicago. He was extradited to the Lake County Jail in Crown Point. Dillinger's plane touched down at Midway Airport in Chicago, Illinois, where he was greeted by thirty-two armed Chicago policemen. Dillinger was transported to the Crown Point Jail by a thirteen-car caravan, including twenty-nine Indiana state troopers.

The arraignment of John Dillinger took place in the Halls of Justice on February 9, 1934, presided over by Judge William J. Murray, who set his trial date for March 12. A crowd of spectators watched as Dillinger was escorted to the Crown Point Jail through the "bridge of sighs" that connected the courthouse to the jail. The name "bridge of sighs" comes from the suggestion by Lord Byron in the nineteenth century that prisoners would sigh at their final view of beautiful Venice through the window before being taken down to their cells.

Not even two months after John Dillinger began to occupy a cell at the Crown Point Jail, he executed the plan that would lead to his freedom. On March 3, 1934, while the prisoners were having breakfast in the day room, the main cellblock door was left open by Sam Cahoon, a handyman at the jail. Holding a pistol under his chin, Dillinger forced Cahoon into the cellblock. Herbert Youngblood, an African American prisoner charged with murder, assisted John by threatening prison guard Wildred Bryant with the handle of a toilet plunger and locking him and two trustees into the number two cell. Once in the cellblock, Cahoon was made to lock down the cells and dayroom. Proceeding down a long corridor, Dillinger came upon fingerprint technician Ernest Blunk. After deciding he would rather hold Blunk hostage, he locked Cahoon in a cell and acquired two fully loaded Thompson submachine guns that were sitting on a windowsill in Warden Baker's office. Behaving as if they had all the time in the world, Dillinger, Youngblood and Blunk walked through the courtyard into the garage, where the employees' cars were kept, two buildings north of the Criminal Courts Building.

Reaching the garage, Dillinger asked Edwin Saagar, the garage mechanic, "What's the fastest car you got?" After indicating Sheriff Lillian Holley's new 1933 Model 40 Fort V-8 Tudor, Saager was made to disable two other vehicles and then drive Dillinger and his passengers out of Crown Point and into Illinois and freedom.

On Sunday, July 22, 1934, just over four months after his escape from Crown Point, John Dillinger's luck ran out in front of the Biograph Theatre in Chicago, Illinois. Following a tip from Anna Sage, immortally known as "the lady in red," special FBI agent Melvin Purvis greeted Dillinger with a barrage of gunfire as he was leaving the theater. A fatal shot to the back of his neck ended the life of John Herbert Dillinger, declared Public Enemy No. 1 by the FBI on his birthday, only one month earlier. Dillinger was laid to rest on July 25, 1934, at the Crown Hill Cemetery in Indianapolis.

John H. Dillinger's headstone has been replaced four times due to damage done by souvenir seekers.

Strange noises are continually heard in the cellblock that John Dillinger escaped from over eighty years ago. The clanking of metal on metal that resembles the sounds of cell doors being opened and shut, rattling of cell bars and a quick, repetitious thudding echo can be heard coming from the corridors. Dillinger was said to have dragged the wooden pistol that aided him in his famous escape across the cell bars, mocking the warden after he had locked him inside. Can this still be John, who has ironically never escaped?

On November 6, 1933, psychopath James "Fur" Sammons found himself secured in a cold jail cell in the maximum-security Crown Point Jail. Alleged to be a hit man for Al Capone, he began his criminal career in 1899, when, at sixteen, he was sentenced to the Pontiac reformatory for gang raping and beating an eleven-year-old girl. Two months after his release, he was arrested for the murder of Patrick Barret, convicted and sentenced to receive the death penalty. He escaped in 1917, but by this time, he was considered insane due to his lengthy stay in solitary confinement. After several convictions for robbery and murder, Sammons, released on $20,000 bond, was arrested in Cedar Lake, Indiana, for driving while intoxicated. For twenty-five days, Sammons's evil prevailed while he awaited the eventual sentence of life imprisonment for his habitual criminal activity.

The Crown Point Jail has been the temporary home to many desperate souls charged with ghastly crimes, such as kidnapping, robbery and murder. Does their ominous presence remain embedded in the walls that once confined them?

Entering the sheriff's residence and proceeding through the back door to the jail, one becomes overwhelmed with a sense of dread and melancholy. Accessing the booking area, prisoners were greeted and booked, which officially admitted them to the hospitality of the Crown Point Jail. A female apparition is said to be seen in this area on the stairs.

A large security door separates this more public area from the long stretch of narrow corridor where numerous jail cells equipped with iron bars are lined up in a row. Stories of paranormal activity in this area are abundant. The heavy cell doors have been witnessed to open and close by themselves. Figures of what are believed to be past inmates have made themselves briefly available to tour-goers of the jail. Many people have had the experience of being gently pushed into the cells by unseen hands when standing just at the threshold of the jail cells. Could it be that the prison guards here are on eternal duty?

Several ghostly abnormalities have been caught on camera by local visitors and ghost hunters. Images of a man standing in the window of the jail, looking out over the courtyard, and a woman looking out the upstairs window of the sheriff's house are just two examples of shots taken outside the jail. Inside the jail, photographs have been taken revealing a man looking out from his jail cell, shadow figures and white mists that appear in areas in the back of the jail. Ghostly images have been caught on camera, even during daylight hours. A photographer from the *Hobart Gazette* captured clear images of faces on one of the cell walls.

Electronic voice phenomenon sessions, taken while inside the jail, have uncovered muted voices that sound like conversations and phantom footsteps that seem to be walking back and forth in front of the cells. Paranormal investigators have recorded full phrases by unseen entities, issuing warnings to them and their groups while touring the jail. There have even been reports of hearing a harmonica, like the one John Dillinger played during his stay at the jail.

When touring the jail, one can also expect a more tangible way for the inmates to make it clear that mere guests are not welcome within their eternal prison. Victims of confrontations with the unseen entities at the jail have been grabbed and slammed into the jail cells, as if violent forces remain. Lights and electrical equipment continue to turn on and off on any given day.

The boiler room that was once located at the rear of the jail has been converted to a craft brewery and pizza restaurant. It was in the alleyway of this building that John Dillinger descended a small staircase from the jail and approached the garage to make his famous getaway. Just inside the door of the brewery's tasting room sits the base of the original eighty-foot brick chimney stack once used by the jail's boiler room, making one ever mindful of the significance of the building.

Crown Brewing, at 211 South East Street, opened its doors in June 2008 with between six and nine of its microbrews on tap. The kitchen, once located in the boiler room, began serving a Jail-burger and adorned its walls with a Dillinger WANTED poster and a framed newspaper photo of three men standing with tommy guns beside the jail, under the headline "Jail That Could Not Hold Killer." Whether it is the ghostly spirit of John Dillinger or the many spirits of the convicts who once occupied the boiler room, there is a presence that makes itself known within the building.

Wait staff have encountered cold spots in the upstairs banquet room and office of Carriage Court Pizza, which shares the space with Crown Brewing. One bartender, while closing the brewery, was pushed from behind by an unknown force in the narrow, dimly lit hallway leading from the pizza restaurant to the banquet room. He recalls, "I was closing up, and just two of us were in the building. I always feel like someone is watching me up here and hate coming up alone. I was returning down the hall to the downstairs when something came up behind me and hit me at my knees, pushing me down. I got up and ran to the bar." Other brewery employees have been present when the security system indicates there is someone in the upstairs banquet room, even though they are the only ones present in the building at closing time. Photographs and video taken in this room show slowly moving orbs of light and milky mists near the office door.

After the state law that required the sheriff to reside in a house adjoining the jail was revoked in 1958, the jail was vacated and the sheriff's house was used for offices until 1974. That year, the new county government complex on Main Street was completed, and the offices moved there. Interest in preserving the historic structure in 1987 led to the creation of the Old Sheriff's House Foundation in 1988. The sheriff's house and jail were placed in the National Register of Historic Places in 1989, and one year later, the house was acquired by the Old Sheriff's House Foundation for $13,400. Renovations to the house and jail began in 1990, and with generous donations of labor and materials by the Northwest Indiana Building and Construction Trades Council, significant repairs have been made to reinforce the exterior and improve the interior of the building.

Cold February weather welcomed tradesmen and work crews to Crown Point in 2008. They descended on the sheriff's house and jail in an effort to prepare the buildings, inside and out, for the filming of *Public Enemies*. Based on the book by Bryan Burrough, and starring Johnny Depp as John Dillinger, the movie follows notorious American gangsters such as John Dillinger, Baby Face Nelson and Pretty Boy Floyd during the crime wave of the 1930s. Re-creating Dillinger's escape from the jail, Johnny Depp spent three days filming and walking in the famous footsteps of Dillinger. In an interview commenting on his ghostly experiences, Depp admitted to feeling a strong sense of Dillinger present with him as he was filming. Consequently, he was not spooked, and he said he felt Dillinger was communicating his approval.

Currently, the old sheriff's house and jail are open and available to tour from May to late September, hosted by the Old Sheriff's House Foundation. Ambitious ghost hunters can even spend a private night investigating to their heart's content on organized haunted events. During the Halloween season, the building is converted to a haunted house, bringing brave visitors a little closer to experiencing the ghostly reputation of the jail.

While strolling past the old sheriff's house and jail on Main Street, one cannot help but linger just a little. Some reflect upon the days of the gangster era and the infamous escape by John Dillinger, imagining men dressed in dark suits and wide-brimmed hats and the street lined with classic autos. Others feel the melancholy or desperation of hundreds of men justly or unjustly imprisoned behind the jail's red brick walls. However, it is the curious ghost hunter who stops and searches the dark in the jailhouse windows for just a glimpse of a face, a flicker of light or a slithering shadow. Surely, the spirits that remain in the Crown Point old sheriff's house and jail encourage this behavior and promise not to disappoint.

BIBLIOGRAPHY

Angelfire. "Gypsies Cemetery." Accessed March 3, 2016. www.angelfire.com/theforce/haunted/gypsiescemetery.htm.

Ball, T.H. *Lake County, Indiana from 1834 to 1872. Primary Source Edition.* N.p.: Nabu Press, 2013.

———. "The Sunday Schools of Lake." In *Indiana Authors and Their Books.* N.p.: Wabash College, 1949, 1974, 1981. webapp1.dlib.indiana.edu/inauthors.

Benjamin Franklin History. "Lending Library." www.benjamin-franklin-history.org/lending-library.

Biography. "Andrew Carnegie Biography." Accessed November 2016. www.biography.com/people/andrew-carnegie-9238756#synopsis.

———. "John Dillinger Biography." Accessed October 2016. www.biography.com/people/john-dillinger-9274804.

———. "Lucrezia Borgia Biography." Accessed September 2016. www.biography.com/people/lucrezia-borgia-9220136.

Chicago Tribune. "Crown Point Man Slain, Chicago Gunman Sought." May 10, 1925. archives.chicagotribune.com/1925/05/10/page/1/article/crown-point-man-slain-chicago-gunmen-sought.

CPHS Advanced Placement English Students. *Crown Point Legacy Project.* 7 vols. 2000–08.

Crown Point, City of, trans. *Treasured Memories Crown Point Indiana.* N.p.: Professional Press, 2005.

Crown Point Library. *Crown Point Library Centennial Commemorative Booklet (1908–2008).* N.p., n.d.

———. *Ghost Hunter Findings*. Pamphlet file, October 27, 2009.

Crown Point Register. "Mayor and City Council O.K. High School Project." N.d.

———. "Unearth Human Bones on High School Site." N.d.

Crown Point's Anniversary, 125 Years of Progress (1834–1959). N.p.: Jorbin's Studio, 1959.

Csepiga, Melanie. "Cemetery's Peace Broken by Vandals." nwitimes, July 10, 1996. www.nwitimes.com/uncategorized/cemetery-s-peace-broken-by-vandals/article_28a9d5ba-3d6e-5eaa-a6b0-a939762628d7.html.

Encyclopedia Britannica, eds. "Works Progress Administration." Updated May 13, 2013. www.britannica.com/topic/Works-Progress-Administration.

Encyclopedia of Chicago. "Century of Progress Exposition." Accessed March 2016. www.encyclopedia.chicagohistory.org/pages/225.html.

Erler, Susan. "Building That Housed Crown Point's First Library Sold." nwitimes, January 30, 2014. www.nwitimes.com/news/local/lake/crown-point/building-that-housed-crown-point-s-first-library-sold/article_41e0f551-1ec0-5e56-ad3b-7520b3f190df.html.

———. "New Owner Plans Move into Former C.P. Carnegie Library." nwitimes, March 8, 2014. www.nwitimes.com/news/local/lake/crown-point/new-owner-plans-move-into-former-c-p-carnegie-library/article_73eab06e-99ae-5d6e-9a01-0ea830d80dcb.html.

Genealogy Trails. "Lake County, Indiana Cemeteries Prior to 1873." *Lake County, Indiana from 1834 to 1872*. genealogytrails.com/ind/lake/cemeteryhistory.html.

Gordon, Leon M., II. "Settlements in Northwest Indiana, 1830–1860." *Indiana Magazine of History* 47, no. 1 (1951): 37–52. scholarworks.iu.edu/journals/index.php/imh/article/view/8024/9761.

Granato, Sherri. "Paranormal Encounters with Johnny Depp, Sandra Bullock, & Regis." Linkedin, March 2, 2016. www.linkedin.com/pulse/sandra-bullock-johnny-depp-regis-philbin-joan-crawford-sherri-granato.

Grave Spotlight. "Sally Rand." Accessed March 2016. www.cemeteryguide.com/gotw-rand.html.

Harvey, Christine. "Louis' Bon Appetit Celebrating 25 Years in Crown Point." nwitimes, November 7, 2001. www.nwitimes.com/uncategorized/louis-bon-appetit-celebrating-years-in-crown-point/article_349485ec-9edc-5430-b950-2b3d76109a36.html.

———. "Neighbors Cast Doubts on Myths Surrounding South East Grove Cemetery." *Times*, October 31, 2001.

Hays, J.E.S. "The General Store." Back in My Time: A Writer's Guide to the 19th Century, August 5, 2012. backinmytime.blogspot.com/2012/08/the-general-store.html.

History of Libraries. "Andrew Carnegie (1835–1919) Scotland & United States." eduscapes.com/history/contemporary/1900.htm.

Howat, William Frederick. *A Standard History of Lake County, Indiana, and the Calumet Region*. Vol. 1. Chicago: Lewis Publishing Co., 1915.

Kobler, John. *Capone: The Life and World of Al Capone*. New York: Putnam Publishing Group, 1971.

Lake County Courthouse Foundation. *The Old Lake Court House Review*. N.p., 1981.

Lake County Star. "Committed Suicide." N.d.

Lake Shore Public Media. "Jump in the Lake Jail—Old Crown Point Jail Ghost Tour." YouTube, January 20, 2015. www.youtube.com/watch?v=4J5ftLO8X50.

Matera, Dary. *John Dillinger: The Life and Death of America's First Celebrity Criminal*. Boston: Da Capo Press, 2005.

Mayhan, Joni. "The Willard Library: Most Haunted Library in the U.S.?" The Ghost Diaries. theghostdiaries.com/the-willard-library-most-haunted-library-in-the-u-s.

McKinkay, Archibald. "Cemeteries Are Home to Halloween Ghosts and Legends." nwitimes, October 22, 2010. www.nwitimes.com/news/local/lake/cemeteries-are-home-to-halloween-ghosts-and-legends/article_d58b970e-fe84-5a4f-9c37-902fe3f88584.html.

———. "Death of Crown Point Lawyer Led to Wild Sort of Justice." nwitimes, June 10, 2001. www.nwitimes.com/uncategorized/death-of-crown-point-lawyer-led-to-wild-sort-of/article_4564db7f-6f8c-5f84-913c-42ced0819f15.html.

Meder, Amanda Linette. "How to Sense Spirits, Ghosts, and the Deceased." Accessed November 2016. www.amandalinettemeder.com/blog/sensing-the-deceased-the-5-most-common-ways-to-feel-a-spirit.

Milwaukee Journal. "Heart Attack Kills Basketball Player." December 15, 1975.

Moran, Tom. "Northwest Indiana a Hotbed for Haunted Folklore." Northwest Indiana Life, October 28, 2015. www.nwindianalife.com/entertainment/gatherings/47223-northwest-indiana-a-hotbed-for-haunted-folklore.

Mystic Files. "How Do Places Become Haunted?" September 27, 2010. www.mysticfiles.com/how-do-places-become-haunted.

Oakman, Jake. "Visit the Jailhouse Made Famous by John Dillinger—Open House." Indiana Insider Blog, September 7, 2013. visitindiana.com/blog/index.php/2013/09/07/visit-the-jailhouse-made-famous-by-john-dillinger.

Old Sheriff's House Foundation. Accessed December 2016. www.oldsheriffshouse.org/timeline.html.

Pennsylvania Historical & Museum Commission. "Classical Revival Style 1895–1950." Pennsylvania Architectural Field Guide, accessed November 2016. www.phmc.state.pa.us/portal/communities/architecture/styles/classical-revival.html.

Schmal, Richard C. "The Hallowed Ground of Our Pioneer Ancestors" Pioneer History, *Lowell Tribune*, October 26, 1988.

Schons, Mary. "The Underground Railroad in Indiana." National Geographic Society, May 26, 2011. nationalgeographic.org/news/underground-railroad-indiana.

Schuette-Voss, Maggie. "Funeral Director Job Not for Everyone." *Herald Journal*, July 21, 1997. www.herald-journal.com/archives/1997/funeral.html.

Seeks Ghosts. "The Gypsies' Cemetery." February 24, 2015. seeksghosts.blogspot.com/2015/02/the-gypsies-cemetery.html.

Spiritual Science Research Foundation. "Sixth Sense." Accessed November 2016. www.spiritualresearchfoundation.org/spiritual-research/sixth-sense/what-is-sixth-sense.

Spivak, Diane Krieger. "History Under High School: Pioneers Buried Where Students." nwitimes, June 5, 1994. www.nwitimes.com/uncategorized/history-under-high-school-pioneers-buried-where-students/article_2d23097e-700f-5b43-8ef6-1a4e31137e55.html.

Swisher, Charles W., and Mable Wise. *Crown Point Indiana, 1934–1984, Sesquicentennial: The Hub City*. Crown Point, IN: L.E. Laney & Son, 1984.

Vettel, Phil. "Louis Bon Appetit Has a Way with French Classics." *Chicago Tribune*, June 5, 1992. articles.chicagotribune.com/1992-06-05/entertainment/9202200226_1_french-classics-sauce-veal

Waymer, Jim. "Old Sheriff's House Will Be Preserved in Crown Point." *Chicago Tribune*, August 2, 1997. articles.chicagotribune.com/1997-08-02/news/9708020037_1_house-and-jail-county-jail-john-dillinger.

Wikipedia. "David Swing." Accessed June 2016. en.wikipedia.org/wiki/David_Swing.

———. "1829–51 Cholera Pandemic." Accessed February 2016. en.wikipedia.org/wiki/1829%E2%80%9351_cholera_pandemic.

———. "Frank McErlane." Accessed October 2016. en.wikipedia.org/wiki/Frank_McErlane.

———. "Parts of a Theatre." Accessed May 2016. en.wikipedia.org/wiki/Parts_of_a_theatre.

———. "Will Carleton." Accessed June 2016. en.wikipedia.org/wiki/Will_Carleton.

Willard Library. "Grey Lady Ghost." Accessed November 2016. www.willard.lib.in.us/about_willard_library/ghost.php.

Yokom, Katy. "Louis Le Francais: A Timeless Take on French Cuisine." *Food and Dining Magazine*, September 25, 2013. www.foodanddine.com/louis-le-francais-a-timeless-take-on-french-cuisine.

About the Author

Judith Tometczak has conducted paranormal research for over fifteen years and is the founder of Crown Point Haunted Tours. She continues to investigate hauntings in Indiana, Illinois, Michigan and Wisconsin. Judith is currently living with her husband, David, in Portage, Indiana.

Visit us at
www.historypress.net

This title is also available as an e-book